Classroom-Ready

Number Talks

for 3rd, 4th and 5th Grade Teachers

Classroom-Ready

Number Talks

for 3rd, 4th and 5th Grade Teachers

1,000 Interactive Math Activities That Promote Conceptual Understanding and Computational Fluency

Nancy Hughes

Published in the United States by:
Ulysses Press
P.O. Box 3440
Berkeley, CA 94703
www.ulyssespress.com

ISBN: 978-1-61243-727-9
Library of Congress Control Number: 2017938172

Printed in the United States
10 9 8 7 6 5 4

Acquisitions editor: Casie Vogel
Managing editor: Claire Chun
Editor: Shayna Keyles
Proofreaders: Renee Rutledge, Caety Klingman
Front cover design: Justin Shirley
Cover art: pencil © Ricardo Romero/shutterstock.com; apple © Studio Barcelona/shutterstock.com
Interior design: what!design @ whatweb.com
Layout: Jake Flaherty
Interior art: © Polyudova Yulia/shutterstock.com

Contents

Fractions 98

Decimals 144

Further Reading Opportunities 163

References 165

About the Author 166

Introduction

History of Number Talks

Number talks were initially developed in the 1990s by Kathy Richardson and Ruth Parker in response to a professional development session for teachers. Although they have been around for some time, I didn't learn about number talks until 2010, when a sales representative gave me a complimentary copy of Sherry Parrish's *Number Talks: Helping Children Build Mental Math and Computational Strategies*. At the time, I was looking for a way to support mental math and computational strategies in the math classroom, and Parrish's book provided that needed support.

Much of my work with number talks, including this book, is based on earlier work of Richardson, Parker, and Parrish. Parrish's initial suggestions on setting up a number talk, and in executing an effective number talk, can be easily implemented when working with students in any setting. This book's intent is to provide examples of number talks based on specific reasoning strategies aligned to Common Core math fluency standards. These reasoning strategies include providing support for the struggling learner by suggesting concrete and pictorial representations, as well as abstract mental computational strategies appropriate for the grade level.

Importance of Number Talks

There are many benefits of utilizing number talks on a daily basis. Number talks are a valuable classroom routine for developing efficient computational strategies, making sense of math, and communicating mathematical reasoning. A number talk is structured to help students conceptually understand math without memorizing a set of rules and procedures. Instead, they help students understand numerical relationships, such as by composing (putting together existing numbers) and decomposing (breaking numbers into their subparts), using the base ten system, and learning properties of operations.

The primary goal for a number talk is to improve computational fluency (flexibility with computational methods, ability to explain and discuss a reasoning strategy, and computation with accuracy). Sharing math strategies during a number talk clarifies the student's thinking and helps develop the language of math. Students learn that numbers are made up of smaller numbers that can be composed and decomposed to make new numbers. They have the opportunity to think first and self-correct if needed.

Below are seven great components of a number talk, the first being most important. Number talks should help students:

+ Build computational fluency

+ Continue mental computation practice, which builds fluent retrieval of basic facts

+ Actively engage in learning

+ Focus on number sense and mathematical communication

+ Elicit efficient and accurate computational skills

+ Understand the relationships between numbers by modeling strategies

+ Move from concrete to representational to abstract thinking

If your goal is to improve computational skills, number talks are extremely useful, whether in the classroom, as an intervention, in homeschool settings, or for parents wanting to improve their child's math skills.

Number Talks in the Intermediate Classroom

When? Anytime during the school day; prior to math core instruction; morning work; as a whole group; in a small group; during intervention time

How long? Usually 5 to 10 minutes. It does not replace core instruction

What does this implementation look like?

+ Teacher presents a strategic computational problem

+ Students are given sufficient time to determine a solution; when they have an answer, they signal with a thumbs-up

+ Teacher facilitates by recording student strategies and solutions

+ Students share and explain their solution as the teacher records student strategies

+ Teacher asks key questions to elicit discussion. Teacher is prepared to offer a strategy if needed. Class agrees on the correct solution

Conceptual Understanding Leads to Procedural Fluency

Math is a skill that must be developed over time, and it is essential that basic skills are practiced and reinforced daily. Number talks are a powerful way to enable students to become mathematical thinkers, efficient and accurate with computation, and ready to problem solve.

In order for students to be proficient in their mathematical thinking and reasoning, it is important that they have a strong foundation of conceptual understanding. This knowledge comes from understanding number relationships. Number talks help students see the relationships between numbers by discussing and sharing various computational strategies. Teaching, reviewing, and reinforcing reasoning strategies gives students the tools they need for lifelong learning. Each student will comprehend math differently, so teaching multiple strategies in a variety of ways is necessary for all students to make sense of math.

The number one complaint from teachers is that struggling learners do not know their basic facts and cannot compute or reason with numbers. However, math is built on effort, not ability. Early math deficits have devastating effects on later learning. It is essential for students to understand computation so they will become procedurally fluent. Fluency involves knowing reasoning strategies and when to use them. Students must be not only flexible with numbers, but they must be efficient and accurate as well. For example, counting on fingers is a strategy, but it is not an efficient strategy.

To become fluent, it is essential to have the daily ongoing practice that number talks provide. It is important to move students from concrete to representational to abstract thinking. Number talks can move students from concept learning to understanding the relationships between numbers, then on to recalling facts quickly, efficiently, and accurately.

An important aspect of a number talk is that students articulate and share their strategies. Sharing strategies with other students through a number talk provides the means to explain, justify, and make sense of math.

Below you will see the required fluency standards by grade level. Keep these in mind as you use number talks in whole group, small group, or intervention settings. If students are struggling with a number talk, step back to easier numbers or introduce an easier strategy. If the computation is abstract, consider a representational model or if that is too difficult, use a concrete model.

Grade	Required Fluency according to Common Core State Standards
3	**3.OA.C.7** Fluently multiply and divide within 100, using strategies such as the relationship between multiplication and division (e.g., knowing that if 8 × 5 = 40, 40 ÷ 5 = 8) or properties of operations. By the end of Grade 3, know from memory all products of two one-digit numbers. **3.NBT.A.2** Fluently add and subtract within 1,000 using strategies and algorithms based on place value, properties of operations, and/or the relationship between addition and subtraction.
4	**4. NBT.B.4** Fluently add and subtract multi-digit whole numbers using the standard algorithm.
5	**5. NBT.B.5** Fluently multiply multi-digit whole numbers using the standard algorithm.

The Eight Common Core State Standards for Mathematical Practice

1. Make sense of problems and persevere in solving them.

2. Reason abstractly and quantitatively.

3. Construct viable arguments and critique the reasoning of others.

4. Model with mathematics.

5. Use appropriate tools strategically.

6. Attend to precision.

7. Look for and make use of structure.

8. Look for and express regularity in repeated reasoning.

Addition

"Math is not about numbers or the right answer. Math is about discovery and exploring different ways of thinking. It's about teaching your students that they can solve anything. And giving them the tools to make it possible."

—*Unknown*

In this section are the following addition strategy examples with suggested number talks:

Addition Using Base Ten Blocks

Add: 53 + 32

	Tens	Ones	Solve
53			I have a total of 8 tens, or 80, and I have 5 ones. **80 + 5 = 85** **53 + 32 = 85**
32			

Tip: A number talk should be a short, ongoing daily routine.

QUESTIONS

- How do base ten blocks help visualize addition?

- Do you have another strategy to share?

Add 71 + 51

Tens	Ones

Add 67 + 42

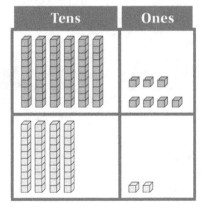

Add 46 + 23

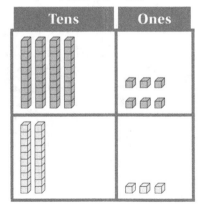

Addition Using Base Ten Blocks with Regrouping

Add: 153 + 38

	Hundreds	Tens	Ones	Solve
153				When I add the numbers in the ones place, I have 11 ones. I can trade 10 ones for 1 ten (and move the new 10 to the tens place). Now, I have 9 tens and 1 one.
38				$100 + 90 + 1 = 191$ $153 + 38 = 191$

Tip: Students share and explain their thinking while the teacher records students' thinking.

QUESTIONS

- What do you see?
- How do base ten blocks help visualize addition?

- Can you explain how to regroup with base ten blocks?
- What would happen if you had 12 tens? How would you regroup?

Add 454 + 236

Hundreds	Tens	Ones

Add 346 + 155

Hundreds	Tens	Ones

Addition with Place Value Strips

EXAMPLE

Add: 562 + 421

Standard Form: | 5 | 6 | 2 | + | 4 | 2 | 1 |

Expanded Form:

| 5 | 6 | 2 | = | 5 | 0 | 0 | + | 6 | 0 | + | 2 |

+ | 4 | 2 | 1 | = | 4 | 0 | 0 | + | 2 | 0 | + | 1 |

| 9 | 0 | 0 | + | 8 | 0 | + | 3 |

562 + 421 = (900 + 80 + 3), or 983

Tip: If a student is struggling with abstract computation, step back to a pictorial or concrete example, such as base ten blocks or place value strips, as shown in this strategy.

QUESTIONS

- Is there another strategy that will help solve this problem?

- Can you show me this using base ten blocks?

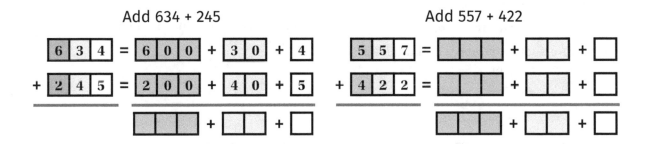

Add 634 + 245

| 6 | 3 | 4 | = | 6 | 0 | 0 | + | 3 | 0 | + | 4 |

+ | 2 | 4 | 5 | = | 2 | 0 | 0 | + | 4 | 0 | + | 5 |

Add 557 + 422

| 5 | 5 | 7 | = | | | | + | | | + | |

+ | 4 | 2 | 2 | = | | | | + | | | + | |

Addition with Place Value Strips and Regrouping

EXAMPLE

Add: 689 + 743

Standard Form: | 6 | 8 | 9 | + | 7 | 4 | 3 |

Expanded Form:

| 6 | 8 | 9 | = | 6 | 0 | 0 | + | 8 | 0 | + | 9 |

+ | 7 | 4 | 3 | = | 7 | 0 | 0 | + | 4 | 0 | + | 3 |

| 1 | 3 | 0 | 0 | + | 1 | 2 | 0 | + | 1 | 2 |

689 + 743 = (1,300 + 120 + 12), or 1,432

Tip: Remind students that we regroup when the numbers we are adding are two digit numbers (10 or more) in the ones column or three digit numbers (100 or more) in the tens columns, etc.

QUESTIONS

- What do you see?
- What is your estimated answer?
- How do you know this is right?
- Is there another strategy that will help solve this problem?

- Was your answer close to the estimated value?
- Can you show me this using base ten blocks?

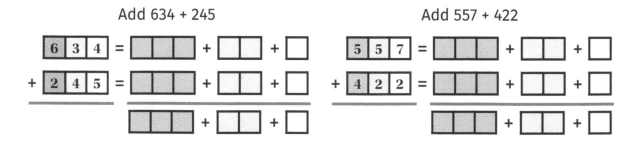

Add 634 + 245

Add 557 + 422

Jumps on a Number Line

What is 36 + 29?

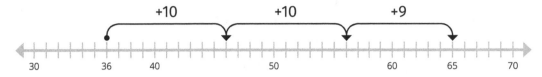

Thus, 36 + 29 = 65

Decompose 29 to 10 + 10 + 9. To find the sum, start with the first addend, 36, on the number line, and jump by 10, then another 10, then by 9.

Tip: For the struggling learner, begin with one-digit numbers or use a strategy such as Making Tens (page 15).

QUESTIONS

- Can you explain how this strategy works?
- How do you know your answer is right?
- Could you have solved this problem in a different way?

Estimate first and be prepared to share your thinking.

29 + 62	31 + 64	39 + 26
44 + 52	56 + 32	17 + 81
26 + 27	43 + 23	38 + 49
64 + 29	76 + 15	53 + 28

Compensation

Add: 47 + 36

(47 + 3) + (36 - 3)

50 + 33

83

Thus, 47 + 36 = 83

To make addition easier, take 3 away from 36 and compensate by adding the 3 to the first addend, 47. Now, you have easier numbers to add: 47 + 3 = 50 and 36 - 3 = 33. Then, add your tens (50 + 30 = 80) and your ones (0 + 3 = 3), and add the sums together (80 + 3 = 83).

Tip: A number talk should be a short, ongoing daily routine.

QUESTIONS

- Can you explain how compensation works?
- Can you prove your answer is correct?
- Do you have another strategy to share?

Estimate first and be prepared to share your thinking.

49 + 53	85 + 49	76 + 38
97 + 64	27 + 18	25 + 27
34 + 12	54 + 29	46 + 31
76 + 55	74 + 28	65 + 57
537 + 46	245 + 88	199 + 33

Making Tens

Add: 88 + 26

(80 + 4 + 4) + (20 + 6)

Then, redistribute the numbers

(80 + 20) + (4 + 6) + (4)

100 + 10 + 4

114

Thus, 88 + 26 = 114

To make addition efficient, look for tens. You can decompose 88 to 80 + 4 + 4 so it can be easily added to 26, which decomposes to 20 + 6. Now you have easy numbers to add when you combine 80 + 20 and 4 + 4 + 6.

Tip: Number talks should focus on number sense, place value, and fluency.

QUESTIONS

• How is adding by tens more efficient?

• Did you use another strategy? Can you share your strategy and thinking?

Estimate first and be prepared to share your thinking.

62 + 28	25 + 87	42 + 87
47 + 66	86 + 25	72 + 54
114 + 27	326 + 46	46 + 65

Landmark Numbers

Add: 48 + 24

(2 + 22)

(48 + 2) + (22)

50 + 22

72

Thus, 48 + 24 = 72

You can make addition easier by decomposing one number and adding it to another. In this example, you can decompose 24 to 2 + 22. Now you can add 2 to 48 to make an easier number to add (50).

Tip: A number talk is mental math, not paper and pencil.

QUESTIONS

- How is the Landmark Numbers strategy similar to and different from Making Tens and Compensation?

Estimate first and be prepared to share your thinking.

49 + 8	67 + 8	78 + 7
48 + 23	19 + 26	55 + 58
91 + 48	218 + 34	97 + 56

Doubles Plus

Add: 48 + 49

(48 + 1)

(48 + 48) + (1)

96 + 1

97

Thus, 48 + 49 = 97

To add these two numbers, look for doubles of 48. Since the second addend is 49, you can decompose 49 to 48 + 1. Now you have doubles to add (48 + 48 = 96). 96 plus the leftover 1 makes 97.

Tip: Through this number talk, students see that numbers can be composed and decomposed to make new numbers.

QUESTIONS

- Is this similar to another strategy you know?
- If you double the second addend, how do you find your solution?

Estimate first and be prepared to share your thinking.

34 + 35	16 + 17	39 + 38
62 + 64	24 + 25	12 + 14
58 + 59	22 + 23	84 + 86

Doubles/Near Doubles

Add: 56 + 58

(56 - 1) (58 - 3)

(55 + 55)

110

110 + (1 + 3) = 114

Thus, 56 + 58 = 114

Look for a set of doubles that are easy to add. Addition by 5 is easy, so you can look for doubles of 55. If you subtract 1 from the first addend and 3 from the second addend, you have 55. Don't forget to add on the numbers you removed (1 + 3).

Tip: Provide problems with various levels of difficultly that can be solved in a variety of ways.

QUESTIONS

- Would it have been easier to add doubles of 55 or 58? Would it have made a difference with the final sum?

- Why do you have to add 1 and 3 after finding these doubles?

Estimate first and be prepared to share your thinking.

24 + 27	52 + 54	81 + 83
66 + 68	48 + 50	76 + 78
58 + 55	214 + 216	96 + 98
37 + 121	169 + 92	314 + 233

Rounding Up or Down

Add: 47 + 38

Round 38 to 40, then add

47 + 40

∨

87

87 - 2

∨

85

Thus, 47 + 38 = 85

To easily add 47 + 38, you round the second addend (38) to 40 by adding 2. Now, it's easy to add 47 + 40 to make 87. Since you added 2 to the second addend, compensate by taking 2 away from the sum of 87. 87 - 2 makes 85.

Tip: Use correct mathematics vocabulary during a number talk.

QUESTIONS

- Could you have rounded 47 to 50 instead of rounding 38 to 40? Would this have changed your sum?

- How do you know whether to add or subtract once you have added your rounded number?

Estimate first and be prepared to share your thinking.

49 + 36	58 + 12	13 + 18
61 + 38	43 + 28	67 + 29
11 + 89	75 + 9	57 + 28

Decomposing Using Place Value

Add: 38 + 26

(30 + 8) + (20 + 6)

Add the tens, then the ones.

(30 + 20) + (8 + 6)

50 + 14

64

Thus, 38 + 26 = 64

Decompose the two addends into their expanded forms. Add the numbers in the tens place, then the numbers in the ones place. Finally, add 50 + 14 to make 64.

Tip: The goal of a number talk is computational fluency and conceptual understanding. Make sure students do not rely on procedures only.

QUESTIONS

- What other strategies does this remind you of?
- Could you use base ten blocks or place value strips to solve this problem?

- Can you repeat the strategy in your own words?
- Do you agree or disagree with the strategy? Why?

Estimate first and be prepared to share your thinking.

47 + 43	18 + 19	62 + 17
457 + 42	168 + 42	46 + 53
883 + 116	372 + 632	188 + 93

Adding Left to Right

Add: 64 + 38

6|4 + 3|8	60 + 30 = 90
6|4 + 3|8	4 + 8 = 12

90 + 12

⌄

102

Thus, 64 + 38 = 102

Begin by adding the numbers in the tens place, then add the numbers in the ones place. Finally, add both sums to get the answer.

Tip: For the struggling learner, begin with one-digit numbers. Use manipulatives like place value strips or base ten blocks if necessary.

QUESTIONS

- Can you explain your strategy and how it works?
- Does anyone else have a strategy that works?
- Could you have solved this problem a different way?
- Explain your thinking.

Estimate first and be prepared to share your thinking.

56 + 25	25 + 48	35 + 39
28 + 51	48 + 42	18 + 57
29 + 18	43 + 24	53 + 37

Adding Smaller Numbers in Expanded Form

Add: 58 + 42

$$
\begin{array}{r}
50 + 8 \\
+\ 40 + 2 \\
\hline
90 + 10 \\
\end{array}
$$

100

Thus, 58 + 42 = 100

Decompose the number to expanded form. Add based on place value.

Tip: As students learn new strategies, add them to your vocabulary wall.

QUESTIONS

- Does adding in expanded form make addition easier? How?

- Does this remind you of any other strategies you've used?

Estimate first and be prepared to share your thinking.

34 + 58	48 + 42	78 + 15
22 + 30	55 + 35	67 + 27
37 + 32	22 + 52	49 + 37
62 + 28	79 + 16	43 + 37
92 + 75	63 + 71	22 + 48

Adding Larger Numbers in Expanded Form

Add: 1,572 + 3,524

1,000 + 500 + 70 + 2

+ 3,000 + 500 + 20 + 4

4,000 + 1,000 + 90 + 6 = 5,096

Thus, 1,572 + 3,524 = 5,096

Decompose the numbers to expanded form. Add based on place value, starting in the thousands place, then the hundreds place, the tens place, and finally the ones place. The sums of these numbers is the sum of 1,572 + 3,524.

Tip: All student responses should elicit wonderful classroom discussions, even if the solutions are not accurate.

QUESTIONS

- Did you use a different strategy to find your solution? What did you do?
- Do you agree or disagree with your classmates' solutions?

Estimate first and be prepared to share your thinking.

456 + 241	632 + 219	138 + 215
438 + 241	825 + 132	327 + 331
663 + 261	6,335 + 2,437	4,256 + 2,662
4,811 + 1,591	6,767 + 1,224	5,009 + 4,273

Adding Numbers Larger Than 1,000 in Expanded Form

Add: 32,284 + 12,535

30,000 + 2,000 + 200 + 80 + 4

+ 10,000 + 2,000 + 500 + 30 + 5

_____

40,000 + 4,000 + 700 + 110 + 9 = 44,819

Thus, 32,284 + 12,535 = 44,819

Decompose the number to expanded form. Add based on place value, moving from the ten-thousands, thousands, hundreds, tens, and ones place. Finally, add the sums of these numbers to find the solution for 32,284 + 12,535.

Tip: For struggling learners, use smaller numbers to add in expanded form.

QUESTIONS

- How does adding in expanded form make addition easier?
- Can you explain this strategy in your own words?
- Do you agree or disagree with the strategy?

Estimate first and be prepared to share your thinking.

8,235 + 457	2,692 + 828	4,691 + 902
1,542 + 3,698	2,451 + 1,528	3,549 + 2,109
6,210 + 1,671	9,999 + 3,503	42,756 + 17,231
26,872 + 12,342	209,909 + 56,035	580,036 + 200,857

Adding Numbers Over 100 on an Open Number Line

Add: 358 + 226

Expanded Form: 200 + 20 + 6

Thus, 358 + 226 = 584

Start with the first addend on the number line. Then, decompose the second addend into expanded form. Jump up the number line by place value, first jumping by 200, then by 20, and finally 6 to find the sum of 358 + 226.

Tip: For struggling learners, start with Jumps on a Number Line.

QUESTIONS

- How does it help you add when you write the second addend in expanded form?
- Is there another way to find the solution?
- Can you explain your thinking?
- What would happen if...?

Estimate first and be prepared to share your thinking.

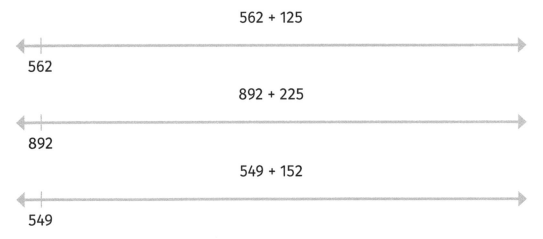

562 + 125

562

892 + 225

892

549 + 152

549

Adding Numbers Over 1,000 on an Open Number Line

Add: 3,567 + 2,121

Expanded Form: 2,000 + 100 + 20 + 1

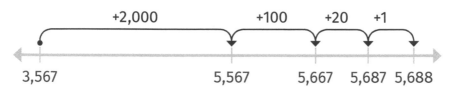

Thus, 3,567 + 2,121 = 5,688

Begin with the first addend, 3,567. Using the second addend in expanded form, jump up by 2,000 on the number line, then by 100, then by 20, and finally by 1 to find your solution.

Tip: For struggling learners, use smaller numbers. Start with Jumps on a Number Line then move up to Adding Numbers Over 100 on an Open Number Line.

QUESTIONS

- How does using the expanded form make it easier to add?
- What number do you start with on the open line?
- Do you disagree with the strategy used? Do you have an easier strategy?

Estimate first and be prepared to share your thinking.

12,525 + 1,645

29,872 + 20,229

1,674 + 1899

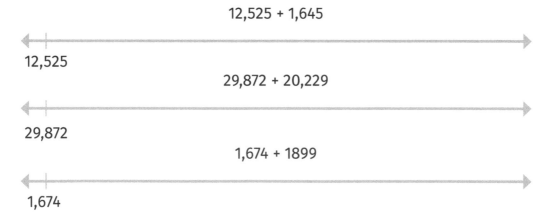

Adding Based on Partial Sums

Add: 32,284 + 12,535

$$
\begin{array}{r}
32,284 \\
+ \ 12,535 \\
\hline
40,000 \\
+ \ 4,000 \\
700 \\
110 \\
9 \\
\hline
44,819 \\
\end{array}
$$

Thus, 32,284 + 12,535 = 44,819

Decompose based on place value. Add the values from left to right, like in the exercise on page 21. Add the numbers in the ten-thousands place (30,000 + 10,000). Next add the thousands place (2,000 + 2,000). Now add the numbers in the hundreds place (200 + 500), tens place (80 + 30), and finally the ones place (4 + 9). Finally, add all the partial sums to find the total sum.

Tip: Make sure students find a strategy before giving you a thumbs up.

QUESTIONS

- Can you get the correct answer if you add left to right instead of right to left?
- Can you explain why this strategy works?
- Is this strategy similar to another strategy we used?
- Was your estimate answer close to the actual value?

Estimate first and be prepared to share your thinking.

356 + 211	764 + 215	7,851 + 920
6,286 + 3,213	7,779 + 2,352	753,118 + 105,116

Finding Perimeter by Adding Lengths

What is the perimeter of this shape?

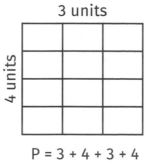

3 units

4 units

P = 3 + 4 + 3 + 4

P = 14 units

Perimeter is the sum of the length of each side. You can find the perimeter of this shape by adding the side lengths.

Tip: For the struggling learner, use a concrete model (geoboard or color tiles) and have students count the side lengths.

QUESTIONS

- What strategy did you use to add? Explain.
- What would happen if you double the sides and add?

- Will you get the same answer if you add the two sides and then double the answer?

What is the perimeter?

4 units

7 units

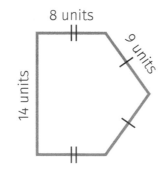

8 units

14 units

9 units

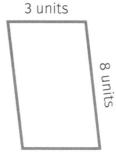

3 units

8 units

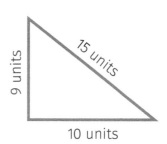

9 units

15 units

10 units

Subtraction

"I could never have gone far in any science because on the path of every science, the lion Mathematics lies in wait for you."

— *C. S. Lewis*

STANDARDS

3.NBT.A.2 Fluently add and subtract within 1,000 using strategies and algorithms based on place value, properties of operations, and/or relationship between addition and subtraction.

4.NBT.B.4 Fluently add and subtract multi-digit whole numbers using the standard algorithm.

4.MD.C.7 Recognize angle measure as additive. When an angle is decomposed into non-overlapping parts, the angle measure of the whole is the sum of the angle measures of parts. Solve addition and subtraction problems to find unknown angles on a diagram in real-world and mathematical problems.

In this section are the following subtraction strategy worksheets:

Subtracting Using Base Ten Blocks

Subtract: 58 - 32

	Tens	Ones	Solve
58			58 has a value of 5 tens and 8 ones. 32 has a value of 3 tens and 2 ones. Here, you need to take away 3 tens and 2 ones from 58. Removing 2 ones from 8 ones leaves 6 ones, and removing 3 tens from 5 tens leaves 2 tens. Thus, **58 - 32 = 26**
32			

Tip: Have students listen to their classmates' responses and discuss each one respectively.

QUESTIONS

• How do base ten blocks help visualize subtraction?

• How does this relate to addition?

Subtract 74 - 52

Tens	Ones

Subtract 57 - 32

Tens	Ones

Subtract 49 - 26

Tens	Ones

Subtracting Using Base Ten Blocks with Regrouping

EXAMPLE

Subtract: 163 - 58

	Hundreds	Tens	Ones	Solve
163				In order to take 8 ones away from 3 ones, you need to trade a ten for 10 ones. Now you have 13 ones. 6 tens and 3 ones is the same as 5 tens and 13 ones. It is now easy to take 8 ones away from 13 ones. So 13 - 8 = 5 ones. Thus, **163 - 58 = 105**
58				

Tip: Teach students to respect each other's discussion points.

QUESTIONS

- What do you see?
- Can you explain how regrouping with base ten blocks works?
- Does this help you visualize subtraction? How?

Subtract 454 - 236

Hundreds	Tens	Ones

Subtract 346 - 155

Hundreds	Tens	Ones

Subtracting with Place Value Strips

Subtract: 862 - 421

Standard Form: | 8 | 6 | 2 | - | 4 | 2 | 1 |

Expanded Form:

| 8 | 6 | 2 | = | 8 | 0 | 0 | + | 6 | 0 | + | 2 |

| - | 4 | 2 | 1 | = | 4 | 0 | 0 | + | 2 | 0 | + | 1 |

| 4 | 0 | 0 | + | 4 | 0 | + | 1 |

Thus, 862 - 421 = (400 + 40 + 1), or 441

Tips: For struggling learners, use manipulatives, such as base ten blocks or place value strips, as shown in this strategy.

QUESTIONS

- What is your estimated answer?
- How do you know your answer is right?
- Is there another strategy that will help solve this problem?

- Can you show how to solve this problem using base ten blocks?

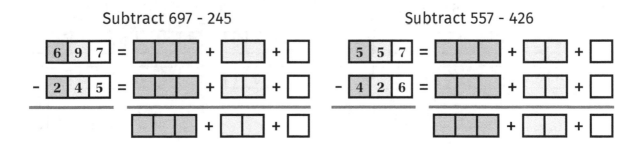

Subtract 697 - 245

Subtract 557 - 426

Subtracting Using Place Value Strips and Whether to Use Regrouping

EXAMPLE

Subtract: 824 - 589

Standard Form:

| 8 | 2 | 4 | - | 5 | 8 | 9 |

Expanded Form:

| 8 | 2 | 4 | = | 8 | 0 | 0 | + | 2 | 0 | + | 4 |

| - | 5 | 8 | 9 | = | 5 | 8 | 9 |

| 2 | 1 | 1 | + | 2 | 0 | + | 4 |

Thus, 824 - 589 = (211 + 20 + 4), or 235

Since there are not enough tens or ones (20 + 4) to subtract 8 tens and 9 ones (80 + 9), do not expand 589. Subtract 589 from 800.

Tip: Students can defend or disprove a strategy, as long as it is done respectfully.

QUESTIONS

- Is there another strategy that will help solve this problem?

- Why did you not expand 589?

- Can you show how to solve this problem using base ten blocks?

Subtract 857 - 563   Subtract 262 - 181

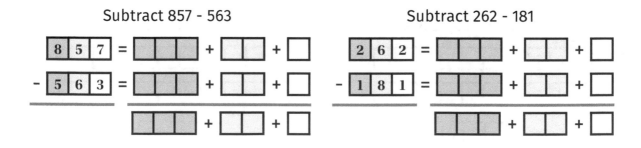

Adding Up to Subtract

EXAMPLE

Subtract: 78 - 42

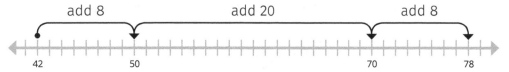

The distance between 42 and 78 is 8 + 20 + 8, or 36.

Thus, 78 - 42 = 36

Using a number line, subtract numbers by adding the distance between them. Starting with 42, the subtrahend, add 8 to get to 50. Adding 20 will take you to 70, and adding another 8 will take you to 78. Add up the distance between the two numbers to find the difference: 8 + 20 + 8 = 36. Therefore, 78 - 42 = 36.

Tip: Use questioning to help students refine, clarify, and make sense of math.

QUESTIONS

• How does this strategy work?

• Is there another similar strategy that helped you?

Estimate first and be prepared to share your thinking.

85 - 38	54 - 28	63 - 25
86 - 37	75 - 29	52 - 27
45 - 17	64 - 48	69 - 52
51 - 29	77 - 27	94 - 18

Counting Back

Subtract: 78 - 42

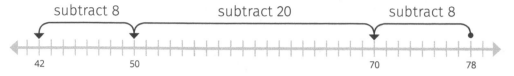

subtract 8   subtract 20   subtract 8

42   50   70   78

The distance between 42 and 78 is 8 + 20 + 8, or 36.

Thus, 78 - 42 = 36

Using a number line, you can subtract numbers by adding the distance between both numbers. Instead of adding up from 42, count back from 78, jumping by groups of tens and ones.

Tip: A number talk is mental math, and should not require paper and pencil.

QUESTIONS

- How does this strategy work? Can you explain this?

- How is this similar to the Adding Up to Subtract strategy?

Estimate first and be prepared to share your thinking.

19 - 14	88 - 52	59 - 35
38 - 24	97 - 63	58 - 41
77 - 48	332 - 218	47 - 25
544 - 136	189 - 175	274 - 116

Counting Back by Hundreds, Tens, and Ones

Subtract: 425 - 161

(100 + 10 + 10 + 10 + 10 + 10 + 10 + 1)

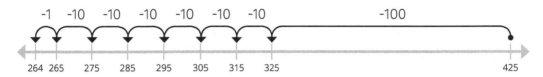

Thus, 425 - 161 = 264

Begin with the minuend and subtract by one hundred, tens, and ones to get the answer. 161 in expanded form is 100 + 60 + 1. Beginning with 425, subtract 100, 6 tens, and 1 one to arrive at a difference of 264.

Tip: For struggling learners, use manipulatives such as base ten blocks or place value strips to show the subtraction. Begin with much smaller numbers.

QUESTIONS

- How is this strategy similar to Adding Up to Subtract?
- How does your answer compare with your estimate?
- How does counting back by hundreds, tens, and ones work?

Estimate first and be prepared to share your thinking.

358 - 143	452 - 132	647 - 124
288 - 142	345 - 225	556 - 153
298 - 154	573 - 245	389 - 214

Decomposing Using Place Value

Subtract: 72 - 48

(70 + 2) - (40 + 8)

Subtract the tens, then the ones.

(70 - 40) + (2 - 8)

30 + (2 - 8)

(20 + 10) + (2 - 8)

20 + (10 + 2 - 8)

20 + (12 - 8)

20 + 4

24

Thus, 72 - 48 = 24

Decompose the minuend and subtrahend into expanded form. First, subtract the numbers in the tens place (70 - 40 = 30). Since you do not have enough ones to do subtraction, trade the 30 tens for 2 tens and 10 ones. Add the 10 ones to the 2 ones to make 12, and now you can subtract 12 - 8.

Tip: Use a thumbs-up approach to give students time to think about the problem and find a strategy to solve the problem.

QUESTIONS

- What would you do differently?
- How do you know this strategy will work?
- Can you repeat the strategy in your own words?
- Do you agree or respectfully disagree with the strategy? Why?

Estimate first and be prepared to share your thinking.

76 - 24	88 - 49	47 - 31
564 - 23	97 - 54	113 - 75

Compensation

Subtract: 73 - 46

(73 + 3) - 46   Compensate.

30 - 3 = 27

76 - 46

30

Thus, 73 - 46 = 27

To make subtraction easier, compensate to give the ones place of the minuend and the subtrahend the same value. Decide which is easier, changing the ones place to 3 ones or 6 ones. In this example, it makes more sense to add 3 to 73 so you can easily subtract 46 from 76. Subtract 76 - 46 to get to 30. Now, compensate by taking the 3 you initially added and removing it from 30.

Tip: It takes time for students to become proficient with number talks.

QUESTIONS

• What other strategies does this make you think of?

• How does this relate to addition?

Estimate first and be prepared to share your thinking.

59 - 38	68 - 47	49 - 12
62 - 49	78 - 32	82 - 64
92 - 76	66 - 29	52 - 19
23 - 14	84 - 57	47 - 28

Round the Subtrahend and Compensate

Subtract: 95 - 47

Round 47 to 50, then subtract.

95 - 50 = 45

Compensate.

45 + 3 = 48

Thus, 95 - 47 = 48

To make subtraction easier, round the subtrahend to the nearest 10 (50). Now subtraction is easy (95 - 50 = 45). Because you increased the distance by adding 3 to the subtrahend, you must compensate by increasing the difference by 3.

Tip: Have students share strategies with a partner before sharing with the class.

QUESTIONS

- How is this similar to Compensation?
- What if you had rounded the minuend?
- How does this work?
- What would you do differently?

Estimate first and be prepared to share your thinking.

27 - 18	64 - 18	23 - 19
49 - 38	36 - 27	78 - 27
51 - 38	93 - 58	75 - 49
64 - 26	75 - 48	49 - 25

Place Value with Small Numbers

Subtract: 72 - 35

(30 + 5)

72 - **3**0 = 42

42 - **5** = 37

Thus, 72 - 35 = 37

Begin by writing 35 in expanded form. Now, subtract the 3 tens and 5 ones in two steps. Start by subtracting the 3 tens (72 - 30 is 42), and then subtracting the five ones (5) from 42 to get a final answer of 37.

Tip: Number talks are a valuable classroom routine for making sense of math, developing computational strategies, communicating thinking, and finding solutions to problems.

QUESTIONS

- How does expanded form help you subtract numbers?
- What would you do differently?
- What answer did you get?

Estimate first and be prepared to share your thinking.

89 - 25	47 - 24	67 - 43
52 - 38	73 - 58	94 - 76
98 - 69	51 - 26	53 - 17
64 - 26	75 - 48	49 - 25

Place Value with Larger Numbers

Subtract: 246 - 154

(100 + 50 + 4)

246 - 100 = 146

146 - 50 = 96

96 - 4 = 92

Thus, 246 - 154 = 92

Begin by subtracting the hundred (246 - 100). Next, subtract the tens (146 - 50). Finally, subtract the ones (96 - 4).

Tip: Number talks help build fluent retrieval of basic math facts.

QUESTIONS

- How does writing a number in expanded form help with subtraction?
- Is this similar to another strategy you've learned? How?

Estimate first and be prepared to share your thinking.

538 - 165	623 - 418	181 - 104
371 - 153	259 - 118	724 - 515
921 - 436	286 - 152	881 - 527
558 - 278	442 - 219	748 - 382

Distance on a Number Line

Subtract: 74 - 28

Adding 2 to both numbers gives you easier numbers to work with.

$$(74 + 2) - (28 + 2)$$

$$76 - 30 = 46$$

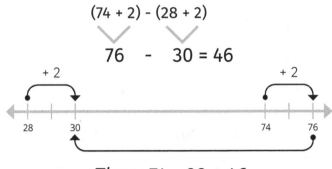

Thus, 74 - 28 = 46

Add 2 to both the subtrahend and minuend, because changing 28 to 30 makes subtraction easier. This just shifts the numbers on the number line. It keeps the distance, or difference, the same. Notice that the distance from 28 to 74 is the same as the distance from 30 to 76.

Tip: Through explanations, students should be making connections with real-world applications.

QUESTIONS

• Why does adding the same number to both subtrahend and minuend keep the solution the same in a subtraction problem?

• Can you explain this in your own words or with an illustration?

Estimate first and be prepared to share your thinking.

26 - 17	38 - 27	57 - 39
63 - 48	41 - 36	75 - 58
53 - 28	28 - 18	37 - 19

Distance on a Number Line: Another Look

Subtract: 1,000 - 579

(1,000 - 1) (579 - 1)

999 - 578 = 421

Thus, 1,000 - 579 = 421

Not only can you add the same number to both subtrahend and minuend, but you can also subtract the same number from the subtrahend and minuend. The distance, or difference, between the two numbers remains the same. In other words, the distance from 1,000 to 579 is the same as the distance from 999 to 578. Regrouping is not an issue here!

Tip: Look for patterns and use properties of operations.

QUESTIONS

- Why does this work?
- How does this strategy help you visualize subtraction?
- Was your estimate close to your actual answer?

Estimate first and be prepared to share your thinking.

900 - 347	800 - 128	1,000 - 598
800 - 592	700 - 124	2,000 - 743
500 - 327	900 - 848	3,000 - 683

Subtracting in Expanded Form

EXAMPLE

Subtract: 56,369 - 34,436

$$50,000 + 6,000 + 300 + 60 + 9$$

$$- \; 30,000 + 4,400 + 000 + 30 + 6$$

$$\overline{20,000 + 1,600 + 300 + 30 + 3}$$

Thus, 56,369 - 34,436 = 21,933

You can subtract these numbers using expanded form. Notice that you will not have enough hundreds (300 - 400), so instead you can move the 400 over to the thousands place and place 000 in the hundreds place. Now you can subtract 4,400 from 6,000.

Tip: Help students see the multiple ways of solving a problem.

QUESTIONS

- Can you share your strategy?
- How does your strategy work?

- Does anyone else have another strategy they want to share?

Estimate first and be prepared to share your thinking.

1,964 - 843	8,969 - 3,327	7,893 - 2,471
9,587 - 6,266	4,854 - 2,611	6,785 - 4,463
19,756 - 7,343	24,769 - 12,528	37,875 - 15,641
56,879 - 23,415	48,968 - 8,546	69,478 - 37,265

Subtracting Smaller Numbers on a Number Line

Subtract: 654 - 365

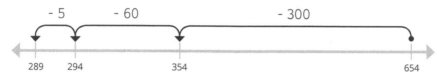

(300 + 60 + 5)

- 5   - 60   - 300

289   294   354   654

Thus, 654 - 365 = 289

Write the subtrahend in expanded form. Begin with the minuend 654 on an open number line. Jump back 3 hundreds to 354. Next, jump back 6 tens to 294, and finally 5 ones to the final answer, 289.

Tip: Celebrate thinking and understanding rather than answer-getting.

QUESTIONS

- What do you see?
- How does expanded form help you subtract numbers?

- Do you have another strategy to share? Can you explain?
- How do you know this strategy will work?
- Do you agree with this strategy? Why?

Estimate first and be prepared to share your thinking.

957 - 726	458 - 237	898 - 683
589 - 367	947 - 116	489 - 175
995 - 831	676 - 115	847 - 717

Subtracting Larger Numbers on a Number Line

Subtract: 25,785 - 23,059

$$(20,000 + 3,000 + 50 + 9)$$

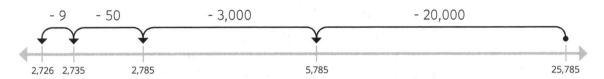

Thus, 25,785 - 23,059 = 2,726

Start with the minuend 25,785 on an open number line and jump back to the answer based on the expanded form of the subtrahend. Starting with 25,785, jump back 2 ten-thousands to 5,785. Next jump back 3 thousands to 2,785, then 5 tens to 2,735, and finally 9 ones to the solution, 2,726.

Tip: Keep the mathematical practices in mind during a number talk.

QUESTIONS

- What do you see?
- Can you explain jumps on an open number line?
- Is there another way this could have been solved? Explain.
- How does writing a number in expanded form help with subtraction?

Estimate first and be prepared to share your thinking.

12,525 - 1,645	12,000 - 4,522	55,575 - 42,463
59,852 - 674	51,370 - 12,622	27,383 - 1,672
7,005 - 5,271	45,825 - 6,374	9,284 - 6,321

Part-Part-Whole

48	
26	

I know that 26 + 22 = 48

I know that 22 + 26 = 48

Thus, 48 - 26 = 22 and 48 - 22 = 26

Identify related facts to determine a missing part or find the whole. You can see that 48 is the whole and 26 is one of the parts. The missing part must be a value that, when added to 26, makes 48. 26 + 20 is 46, and 2 more ones will equal 48. The missing part is 20 + 2, or 22.

Tip: For struggling learners, use smaller numbers. You might want to use this method as an introduction to subtraction.

QUESTIONS

• What strategy can you use to find the missing part?

• How can you check your answer?

• Why did you select that strategy?

Estimate first and be prepared to share your thinking.

34	28

76	
	47

65	18

89	
24	

65	18

88	
28	

52	43

99	
19	

44	22

Finding Missing Angles

EXAMPLE

What's my angle?

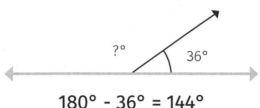

?°   36°

$$180° - 36° = 144°$$

A straight line is 180°. To find the missing angle, you need to subtract 36 from 180 to find the answer. Think of this as a part-part-whole strategy, where 180 is the whole and 36 is one of the parts.

Tip: For struggling learners, try smaller angle measures and simply adding angles to make 90° or 180° angles. Have students estimate their answer before finding the solution.

QUESTIONS

- What do you see?
- How did you know...?
- How is this similar to part-part-whole?

- How does this work?
- What could you have done differently?

Estimate first and be prepared to share your thinking.

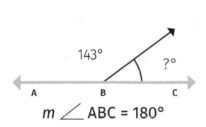

$m \angle$ ABC = 180°

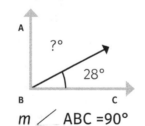

$m \angle$ ABC = 90°

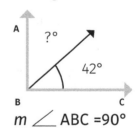

$m \angle$ ABC = 90°

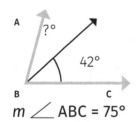

$m \angle$ ABC = 75°

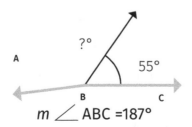

$m \angle$ ABC = 187°

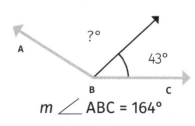

$m \angle$ ABC = 164°

Multiplication

"When you have mastered numbers, you will in fact no longer be reading numbers any more than you read words when reading books. You will be reading meanings."

—*W.E.B. Du Bois*

3.MD.D.8 Solve real-world and mathematical problems involving perimeters of polygons, including finding the perimeter given the side lengths, finding an unknown side length, and exhibiting rectangles with the same perimeter and different areas or with the same area and different perimeters.

4.NBT.B.5 Multiply a whole number of up to four digits by a one-digit whole number, and multiply two two-digit numbers, using strategies based on place value and the properties of operations. Illustrate and explain the calculation by using equations, rectangular arrays, and/or area models.

5.NBT.B.5 Fluently multiply multi-digit whole numbers using the standard algorithm.

5.MD.C.5 Relate volume to the operations of multiplication and addition and solve real-world and mathematical problems involving volume.

In this section are the following multiplication strategy worksheets:

Repeated Addition

Laura has 5 groups of students with 2 students in each group. How many total students are there?

$$5 \times 2 = ?$$

5 + 5 = 10   or   2 + 2 + 2 + 2 + 2 = 10

Thus, 5 × 2 = 10

You can use repeated addition to find the answer. You can view this as 2 groups of 5 or 5 groups of 2.

Tip: This strategy is meant to help emerging learners see the relationship between multiplication and addition. As numbers get larger, this strategy becomes inefficient.

QUESTIONS

- What strategy did you use?
- Is multiplying 5 groups of 2 the same as multiplying 2 groups of 5? Explain your thinking.

- How can you prove your answer?
- How do you know you are right?

Estimate first and be prepared to share your thinking.

5 × 5	9 × 6	7 × 7
7 × 2	6 × 4	6 × 8
8 × 9	10 × 2	5 × 3

Looking for Doubles

EXAMPLE

2 × 5 = ?

⚪ ⚪ ⚪ ⚪ ⚪
⚪ ⚪ ⚪ ⚪ ⚪

2 groups of 5 is 10.

5 doubled is 10.

5 + 5 = 10

Thus, 2 × 5 = 10

If a product of two numbers has a factor of 2, it is the same as a sum of doubles. Doubles should already be a familiar strategy. Start with doubles as a reasoning strategy for multiplication. For example, 2 × 5 is the same as doubling 5.

Tip: If the strategy is difficult, have the student use color counters to show doubles. Drag and drop counters onto a mat and find the product. Or, change to an easier strategy like Repeated Addition.

QUESTIONS

- What is the repeated addition shown?
- 2 groups of _____ is...?

- _____ doubled is...?
- What is 2 × _____?

What is being doubled? What is the total?

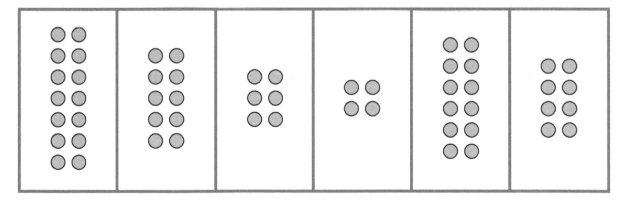

Doubling on a Number Line

EXAMPLE

How many is 2 groups of 6?

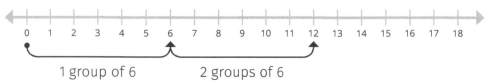

1 group of 6   2 groups of 6

Two groups of 6 is 12.

Thus, 2 × 6 = 12

This is the same as adding 2 groups of 6. You can show this on a number line by starting at 0 and jumping to 6 for the first group of 6, and then jumping another 6 tick marks to 12. 2 × 6 is the same as 12.

Tip: For struggling learners or students having difficulty, step back to using a concrete model with color counters.

QUESTIONS

- What is a double?
- How will a number line help you multiply doubles?

- Can you think of another strategy that will give the same answer?
- How did you find your answer?

Estimate first and be prepared to share your thinking.

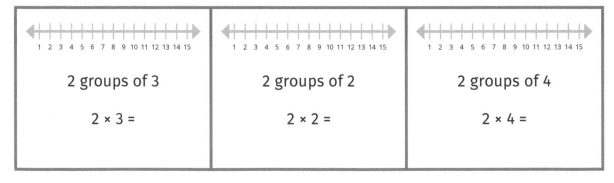

2 groups of 3	2 groups of 2	2 groups of 4
2 × 3 =	2 × 2 =	2 × 4 =

Doubles Plus (3 as a Factor)

3 × 5 = ?

Doubles ⬤⬤⬤⬤⬤ 10
⬤⬤⬤⬤

Plus one set ⬤⬤⬤⬤⬤ 5

2 groups of 5 is 10.

So, 3 groups of 5 is 15.

Thus, 3 × 5 = 15

Think back on your doubles strategy: 2 × 5 = 10. Thus, another set of 5 is 10 + 5, or 15.

Tip: For struggling learners or students having difficulty, step back to using a doubles strategy or Repeated Addition.

QUESTIONS

- How will knowing doubles help with multiplication by 3?
- Can you describe how you used Doubles Plus to find 3 × _____?

- Is this strategy quick and easy to understand?
- Could you use a number line to find the answer?

Estimate first and be prepared to share your thinking.

3 × 2 =	3 × 5
○○ ○○ Double 2	○○○○○ ○○○○○ Double 5
○○ 1 more set	○○○○○ 1 more set
3 × 10	3 × 7
○○○○○○○○○○ ○○○○○○○○○○ Double 10	○○○○○○○ ○○○○○○○ Double 7
○○○○○○○○○○ 1 more set	○○○○○○○ 1 more set

Doubles Plus: Decomposition (Factors of 3)

What is 8 × 3?

(2 + 1)

$$8 \times 2 = 16$$
$$+\ 8 \times 1 = \underline{\ \ 8}$$
$$24$$

Thus, 8 × 3 = 24

Multiply by 3 by first using what you know about doubles (form 2 groups of 8) and then adding on another group of 8. To do this, decompose 3 to addends, 2 and 1. Doubling 8 (by multiplying by 2) will give you 16. Now, all you need to do is add on another set of 8 (by multiplying 8 × 1) to get 24. 8 × 3 is the same as 24.

Tips: For an intervention, step back to either the concrete or representative example, like color counters or a number line, to show multiplication by 3. If you need to step back farther, use doubles of 2 or use Repeated Addition.

QUESTIONS

• Can you describe how decomposing 3 into addends of 2 + 1 helps multiply by 3?

• Do you see another method for multiplying by 3 that works?

• What strategy did you use to multiply by 3?

Estimate first and be prepared to share your thinking.

3 × 9	3 × 6	3 × 8
3 × 11	3 × 13	3 × 15
3 × 12	3 × 21	3 × 32

Doubles Plus Doubles (4 as a Factor)

EXAMPLE

4 × 5 = ?

Double 5

Double again

4 × 5

2 + 2

2 groups of 5 is 10: 2 × 5 = 10.

10 doubled is 20: So, 4 groups of 5 is 20.

Thus, 4 × 5 = 20

If a product has a factor of 4, it is the same as the sum of 2 sets of doubles, or doubling a number and then doubling it again. For example, multiplying 4 by 5 is the same as doubling 5 twice.

Tip: If needed, show Doubles Plus Doubles on a number line. This is a pictorial/ representative format. If you need to step back to a simpler strategy, start with Looking for Doubles or Doubles Plus using factors of 2 or factors of 3.

QUESTIONS

- How can knowing doubles help you multiply by a factor of 4?

- Can you describe how using Doubles Plus Doubles to multiply 4 × 12 works?

Estimate first and be prepared to share your thinking.

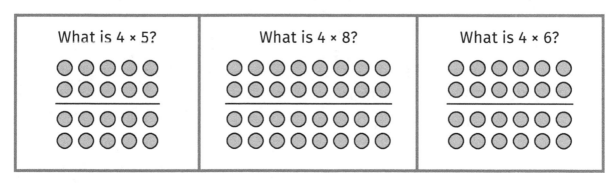

| What is 4 × 5? | What is 4 × 8? | What is 4 × 6? |

Doubles Plus Doubles: Decomposition (4 as a Factor)

What is 7 × 4?

2 + 2

$7 \times 2 = 14$

$+\ 7 \times 2 = 14$

___

28

Thus, 7 × 4 = 28

Break 4 apart to addends 2 + 2. Multiply 7 by both twos. Add the two products. 4 × 7 is the same as (2 × 7) + (2 × 7).

Tip: For an intervention, step back to either the concrete or representative examples by using color counters or a number line. If you need to step back farther, start back with a factor of 2, then 3.

QUESTIONS

- Can you describe how decomposing 4 into addends of 2 + 2 helps multiply by 4?

- Do you see another method of multiplying by 4 that works?

Use decomposition to solve.

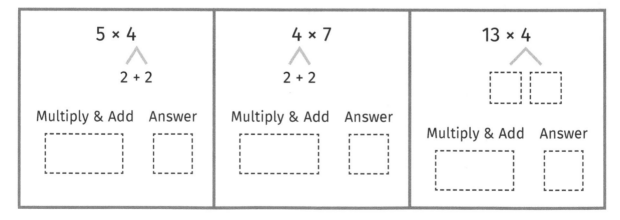

Double, Double, and Double Again (8 as a Factor)

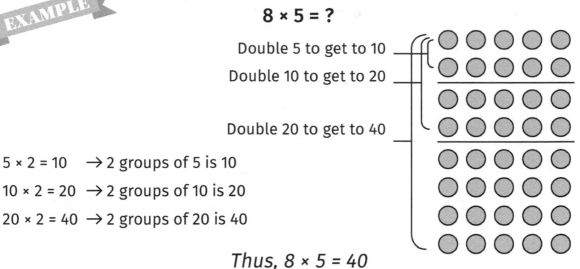

8 × 5 = ?

Double 5 to get to 10

Double 10 to get to 20

Double 20 to get to 40

5 × 2 = 10 → 2 groups of 5 is 10

10 × 2 = 20 → 2 groups of 10 is 20

20 × 2 = 40 → 2 groups of 20 is 40

Thus, 8 × 5 = 40

If a product has a factor of 8, it is the same as the sum of 4 sets of doubles, or doubling a number, then doubling it again, then again.

Tip: Value all responses, even incorrect responses. Give students the opportunity to self-correct errors.

QUESTIONS

- What do you see?
- What strategy is being used?

- Can you think of another strategy that would work?

Double, Double, and Double Again

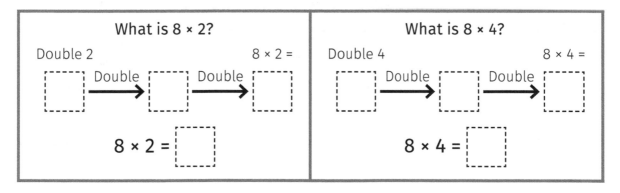

Double, Double, and Double Again: Decomposition (8 as a Factor)

What is 8 × 6?

2 × 2 × 2

2 × 6 = 12

2 × 12 = 24

2 × 24 = 48

Thus, 8 × 6 = 48

Decompose 8 to factors of 2. Multiply 6 by one of these factors to show that 6 × 2 = 12. Double this to show that 6 × 2 × 2, or 12 × 2, is 24. Doubling again shows that 6 × 2 × 2 × 2, or 6 × 8, is 48.

Tip: If students cannot move to this abstract reasoning, step back to a pictorial or concrete representation.

QUESTIONS

- How does multiplying by 2, or using doubles, make multiplication by 8 easier?
- Is there another strategy that you used to get your answer?

- How would this work on a number line or with counters?

Estimate first and be prepared to share your thinking.

8 × 2	7 × 8	8 × 3
8 × 20	8 × 10	8 × 8
12 × 8	8 × 17	8 × 11

Half of 10 (5 as a Factor)

What is 5 × 8?

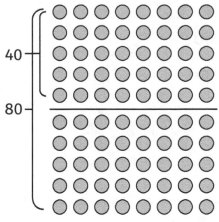

Start with 10 × 8

10 × 8 = 80

↓

Half of 80 = 40

↓

Thus, 5 × 8 = 40

Since you know how to double and half a number, the Half of 10 strategy for multiplying by 5 is easy. The product does not change when you double 5 to 10 and then halve that product.

Tip: If the student cannot visually see half of 10 for a solution, use color counters to prove the answer.

QUESTIONS

- How does multiplying by 10 help you multiply by 5?

- Would it have been easier to decompose 5 to 2 + 2 + 1 to find the solution?

- Do you have another strategy to share?

Estimate first and be prepared to share your thinking.

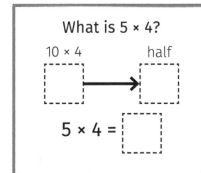

What is 5 × 4?

10 × 4   half

5 × 4 = ☐

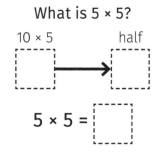

What is 5 × 5?

10 × 5   half

5 × 5 = ☐

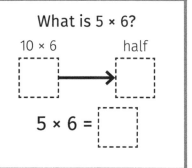

What is 5 × 6?

10 × 6   half

5 × 6 = ☐

Half of 10: Abstract (5 as a Factor)

What is 5 × 12?

Start with 10 × 12 = 120
Half: 120 ÷ 2 = 60

Thus, 5 × 12 = 60

Multiply 12 × 10, which is 120. Half of 120 is 60.

Tip: If the student cannot multiply by 5 abstractly, use color counters.

QUESTIONS

- What strategy did you use to multiply by 5?
- How does knowing how to multiply by 10 help you multiply by 5?
- How does knowing your doubles help you multiply by 5?

Estimate first and be prepared to share your thinking.

5 × 8	5 × 14	5 × 9
12 × 5	5 × 7	5 × 4
16 × 5	20 × 5	5 × 22
5 × 6	30 × 5	5 × 3
44 × 5	5 × 40	24 × 5

Subtracting from 10 (9 as a Factor)

What is 9 × 4?

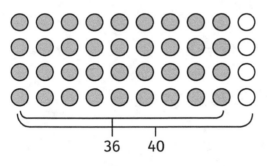

36   40

Start with 10 × 4 = 40

↓

Subtract a set of 4: 40 − 4 = 36

↓

Thus, 9 × 4 = 36

Multiplication by a factor of 9 is easy if you know how to multiply by 10. For example, 9 × 4 is easier if you multiply 10 × 4 first, which gives you 40. 10 groups of 4 is 40, but you only want 9 groups of 4, so you need to remove one group of 4 from 40. 40 - 4 = 36.

Tip: If multiplication by 9 is difficult, use manipulatives or a number line to show the multiplication.

QUESTIONS

- How does multiplying by 10 help you multiply by 9?

- How does this strategy help you multiply by 9?

- Describe the strategy you used to multiply 9 × _____.

Estimate first and be prepared to share your thinking.

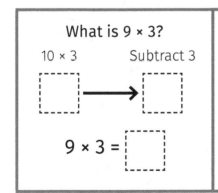

What is 9 × 3?

10 × 3   Subtract 3

9 × 3 =

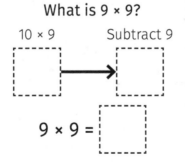

What is 9 × 9?

10 × 9   Subtract 9

9 × 9 =

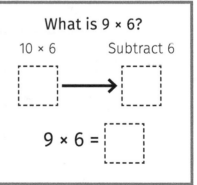

What is 9 × 6?

10 × 6   Subtract 6

9 × 6 =

Subtracting from 10: Abstract
(9 as a factor)

What is 9 × 7?

Start with 10 × 7 = 70
↓
Subtract a set of 7: 70 − 7 = 63
↓
Thus, 9 × 7 = 63

You can visualize 10 groups of 7, or 70. Then remove a group of 7 since you are multiplying by 9 instead of 10.

Tip: Provide wait time for most students to come up with a strategy to solve the problem.

QUESTIONS

- How can multiplying by 10 help you multiply by 9?
- Did you use a different strategy? If so, can you explain your thinking?
- Why do you need to subtract in order to get your answer?

Estimate first and be prepared to share your thinking.

9 × 4	9 × 8	22 × 9
9 × 7	9 × 11	9 × 9
12 × 9	14 × 9	23 × 9

Landmark Numbers

What is 38 × 8?

Make 38 a friendlier number:

38 + 2 = 40

↓

Now multiply:

40 × 8 = 320

↓

Compensate:

2 × 8 = 16

320 − 16 = 304

Thus, 38 × 8 = 304

> Or, put another way:
> (38 × 8) + (2 × 8) = 40 × 8
> Therefore,
> (40 × 8) - (2 × 8) = 38 × 8

Change the 38 to a landmark number, such as 40, by adding 2. Multiply 40 × 8 to get to 320, then adjust the problem by taking away two groups of 8 (2 × 8), or 16, from 320 to get your answer.

Tip: Students should solve the problem mentally before putting their thumbs up to indicate they have a strategy. Provide enough wait time.

QUESTIONS

- Does it matter which number you make into a friendly, or landmark, number?
- Can you prove your answer?

- Why do you have to compensate to get the right answer?
- What would you need to do if you rounded 38 to 30? How would you compensate?

Estimate first and be prepared to share your thinking.

32 × 9	9 × 26	25 × 9
4 × 149	23 × 8	17 × 19
7 × 38	5 × 19	4 × 149

Multiplying Using a Number Line

EXAMPLE Molly has 5 gift boxes. Molly placed 3 basketballs
in each of the 5 boxes. How many total basketballs does she have?

What is 5 × 3?

5 groups of 3

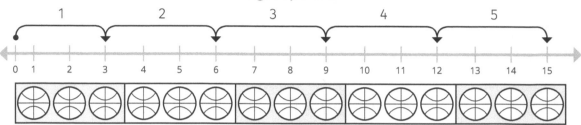

Molly has 15 basketballs total.

Tip: Call on three or four students to share their strategies.

QUESTIONS

• How does a number line help you multiply these numbers?

• Do you agree with the strategy given? Can you state it in your own words?

Estimate first and be prepared to share your thinking.

Alex and his father planted a tree garden. They have 4 rows with 3 trees in each row. How many trees did they plant?

Mr. Smith wants to bake 6 cakes for school. Each cake takes 2 cups of flour. How much flour will Mr. Smith need?

Eli's class went on a field trip. The students traveled in 3 vans. There were 7 students per van. How many students went on the trip?

Natalie is putting pictures in her album. She puts 3 rows of pictures on each page. Each row will hold 3 pictures. How many pictures are on each page?

Doubling and Halving

What is 25 × 16?

	Double:		Half:
25 × 16 =	50	×	8
	100	×	4
	200	×	2

200 × 2 = 400

Thus, 25 × 16 = 400

Double one factor and halve the other factor. Keep doubling and halving until you reach an easy set of numbers to multiply.

Tip: Encourage students to use the language of mathematics.

QUESTIONS

- How does doubling and halving work?
- Are there factors that make halving and doubling difficult? Is this always a good strategy?
- Is one number better than the other for halving or doubling?

Estimate first and be prepared to share your thinking.

5 × 16	4 × 24	5 × 36
15 × 16	35 × 16	50 × 12
18 × 40	12 × 24	7 × 48
43 × 14	26 × 78	68 × 71

Decomposition Using Partial Products

What is 8 × 7?

5 + 2

$8 \times 5 = 40$

$+ 8 \times 2 = 16$

$= 56$

Thus, 8 × 7 = 56

Multiplication is easy if you know your twos, fives, and tens. Pick either factor and decompose it into simpler numbers. Multiplying 8 by 5 and 2 is easier than multiplying by 7.

Tip: Decompose one number or the other to make multiplication easier.

QUESTIONS

- Which number did you take apart to make multiplication easier?
- Can you explain your thinking?

- What strategy is the most efficient for solving this problem?
- How does knowing your twos and fives help you multiply quickly and efficiently?

Estimate first and be prepared to share your thinking.

9 × 6	11 × 4	8 × 7
14 × 4	15 × 4	9 × 9
15 × 5	13 × 6	15 × 7
16 × 7	14 × 6	12 × 6

Factor and Factor Again
(Associative Property)

What is 12 × 24?

3 × 2 × 4

$12 × \underline{3} = 36$

$36 × \underline{2} = 72$

$72 × \underline{4} = 288$

$12 (3 × 2 × 4) = 288$

Thus, 12 × 24 = 288

Change 24 into factors of 24 such as 3 × 2 × 4. Now it is easier to multiply using these smaller numbers.

Tip: Try to relate the strategy to another strategy students have used, such as Looking for Doubles and Doubles Plus.

QUESTIONS

- Could you have changed either number into its factors? What about multiplying by 2 × 2 × 2 × 3? Will you get the correct answer?
- Can you prove your answer another way?
- Does anyone else have another strategy they used?

Estimate first and be prepared to share your thinking.

15 × 6	18 × 4	21 × 8
34 × 4	17 × 4	21 × 6
25 × 9	26 × 6	14 × 9

Multiplication Using an Array

What is 5 × 23?

20   +   3

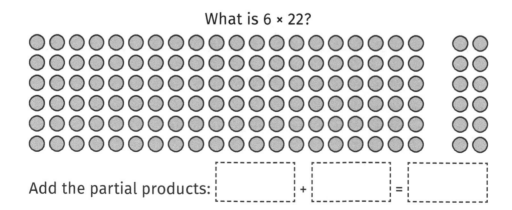

5 × 20 = 100   5 × 3 = 15

Add the partial products:

100 + 15 = 115

Thus, 5 × 23 = 115

Decompose 23 into numbers that are easier to multiply. You now have an array that is 20 by 5 and another that is 3 by 5. 20 × 5 = 100 and 5 × 3 = 15. Add 100 + 15 to equal 115, the solution to 5 × 23.

Tip: Do number talks every day. The more you do a number talk, the better students become at conceptually understanding mathematics.

QUESTIONS

- How can you decompose one of the numbers to make multiplication easier?
- How can you explain your thinking and strategy?
- Does anyone else have another strategy they used to multiply the numbers?
- Do you agree with the strategy used?

What is 6 × 22?

Add the partial products: [   ] + [   ] = [   ]

Multiplication Using an Area Model and Place Value

What is 8 × 346?

	300	+	40	+	6
8	8 × 300 = 2,400		8 × 40 = 320		8 × 6 = 48

Add the partial products:

2,400 + 320 + 48 = 2,768

Thus, 8 × 346 = 2,768

Decompose 346 into numbers based on place value, and multiply 8 by each of the decomposed values. 346 = 300 + 40 + 6.

Tip: For struggling learners, use visuals such as the area model to help them see the partial products.

QUESTIONS

- How can you multiply these numbers using an area model?
- What number did you decompose to find your answer?
- How does an area model help you multiply these numbers?

Estimate first and be prepared to share your thinking.

5 × 58	7 × 86	3 × 45
4 × 57	3 × 52	9 × 81
6 × 164	5 × 341	5 × 3,216

Multiplying 2-Digit Numbers Using an Area Model and Place Value

What is 32 × 25?

	30	+	2
20	30 × 20 = 600		20 × 2 = 40
+			
5	5 × 30 = 150		5 × 2 = 10

Add the partial products:

600 + 40 + 150 + 10 = 800

Thus, 32 × 25 = 800

Decompose 32 and 25 into numbers based on place value: 30 + 2 and 20 + 5. Multiply 20 × 30, 20 × 2, 5 × 30, and 5 × 2. Then, add the partial products to find the total product.

Tip: If a mistake is suggested, allow the student to revise their initial answer.

QUESTIONS

- How can you multiply these numbers using an area model?
- Does this make multiplication easier?
- Where would you place the answer on a number line?

Estimate first and be prepared to share your thinking.

28 × 51	16 × 92	73 × 29
74 × 31	23 × 17	42 × 15
91 × 14	83 × 73	28 × 22

Finding Perimeter Using
$P = 2l + 2w$ or $P = 2(l + w)$

What is the perimeter of this shape?

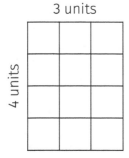

3 units

4 units

$P = (2 \times 3) + (2 \times 4)$

$P = 6 + 8$

$P = 14$ units

or

$P = 2 \times (3 + 4)$

$P = 2 \times 7$

$P = 14$ units

Find the perimeter by multiplying length and width by 2, or by adding the length and width and multiplying by 2.

Tip: For the struggling learner, use a concrete model, like a geoboard or color tiles, and have students count the side lengths. You can also step back and simply add all sides to find the perimeter.

QUESTIONS

• What would happen if you double each of the sides that are labeled and add them together?

• Will you get the same answer if you add the two sides and then double the answer? Why does this work?

What is the perimeter of these shapes?

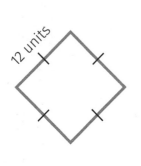

12 units

33 units

81 units

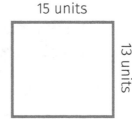

15 units

13 units

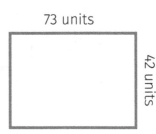

73 units

42 units

Area: *A* = *lw*

What is the area of this shape?

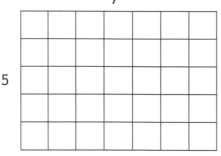

$A = l \times w$

$A = 5 \times 7$

$A = 35$

To find the area of this shape, you could count all the squares that make up the shape, or you could multiply the length by the width.

Tip: For a struggling learner, have them use color tiles, a geoboard, or geobard paper to construct the shape. Have the student count the squares that make up the shape to find the area.

QUESTIONS

- How can you find the area of this shape without counting the squares that make up the shape?

- What strategy did you use to find the area of this shape?
- Would anyone like to share a different strategy?

What is the area of each shaded region?

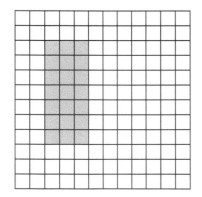
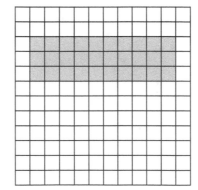
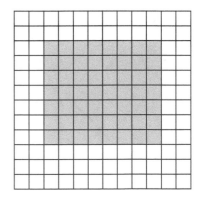

Adding Areas: $A = lw$

Jackie decided to pen in her horse and llama
using connecting pens. How much total area will both animals use?

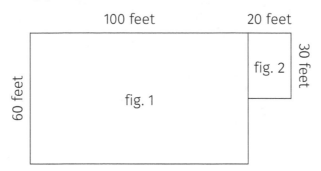

Figure 1 area: $l \times w$ = 100 × 60 = 6,000 feet^2

Figure 2 area: $l \times w$ = 30 × 20 = 600 feet^2

Total area = fig. 1 area + fig. 2 area = 6,000 + 600 = 6,600 feet^2

How can you find the total area of a figure that is composed of more than one shape?
Decompose the shape into non-overlapping rectangles and then add the areas.

Tip: If needed, step back to shapes that do not consist of compound shapes.

QUESTIONS

- What strategy did you use to find the area of this shape?

- Why is it important to decompose the shape before finding the total area?

What is the area of each shaded region?

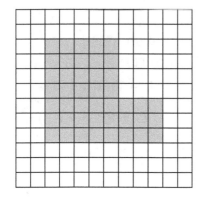
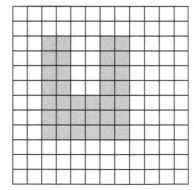
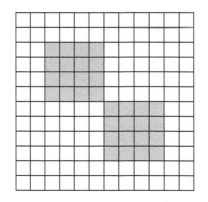

Area and the Distribution Property

What is the area of a rectangle that is 4 feet by 14 feet?

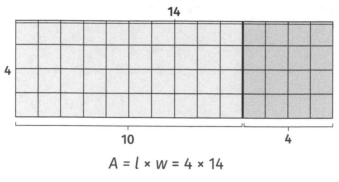

$$A = l \times w = 4 \times 14$$

$$14 = 10 + 4$$

$$A = (4 \times 10) + (4 \times 4)$$

$$A = 40 + 16$$

$$A = 56$$

Thus, the area is 56 feet²

To find the area of this figure, decompose one of the sides to numbers that are easier to work with (in this instance, 14 decomposes to 10 and 4). Find the partial areas using the smaller numbers, and add them together to find the total area.

Tip: For advanced learners, remove the visual cue of a divided shape.

QUESTIONS

• How can you find the area by partitioning the shape into two different shapes?

• How does this make finding the area easier?

Find the area of the figure below by partitioning the shapes based on place value and the distributive property.

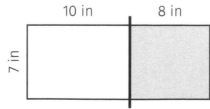

Distributive Property

$(7 \times 10) + (7 \times 8) =$

Area

Volume

What is the volume of a shape that is 3 units by 3 units by 3 units?

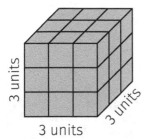

3 units

3 units

3 units

$$V = l \times w \times h$$
$$V = 3 \times 3 \times 3$$
$$V = 27 \text{ units}^3$$

or

$$V = A \times h$$
$$V = 9 \times 3$$
$$V = 27 \text{ units}^3$$

Volume is the number of cubes that will fit into a shape. Volume is measured using the formula **V = lwh** or **V = Ah**. Instead of counting all the cubes that fit into the shape, multiply the length by the width and height. Or, you could find the area of the base shape and multiply that by the height.

Tip: If multiplication is a problem, step back to multiplication by twos, fours, fives, and tens.

QUESTIONS

- What strategy did you use to find the volume of the shape?
- How can you use manipulatives to prove the volume of the shape?

- What does volume tell us?
- Can you describe, in words, how to find volume in two different ways?

What is the volume of each shape?

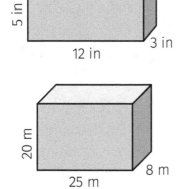

5 in

12 in

3 in

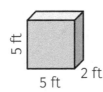

5 ft

5 ft

2 ft

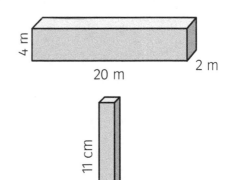

4 m

20 m

2 m

20 m

25 m

8 m

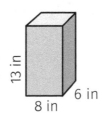

13 in

8 in

6 in

11 cm

2 cm

1 cm

Division

"Math requires repeated experiences with reasoning strategies and not [with] memorization. Fluency is based on understanding these facts. Repeated practice leads to automation and fluency. Reasoning strategies for division include knowing multiplication and applying multiplication to division."

—John Van De Walle

STANDARDS

3.OA.A.4 Determine the unknown whole number in a multiplication or division equation relating three whole numbers.

3.OA.B.5 Apply properties of operations as strategies to multiply and divide.

3.OA.C.7 Fluently multiply and divide within 100, using strategies such as the relationship between multiplication and division (e.g., knowing that if 8 × 5 = 40, 40 ÷ 5 = 8) or properties of operations. By the end of Grade 3, know from memory all products of two one-digit numbers.

4.NBT.B.6 Find whole-number quotients and remainders with up to four-digit dividends and one-digit divisors, using strategies based on place value, the properties of operations, and/or the relationship between multiplication and division.

Illustrate and explain the calculation by using equations, rectangular arrays, and/ or area models.

4.MD.A.3 Apply the area and perimeter formulas for rectangles in real-world and mathematical problems.

5.NBT.B.6 Find whole-number quotients of whole numbers with up to four-digit dividends and two-digit divisors, using strategies based on place value, the properties of operations, and/or the relationship between multiplication and division. Illustrate and explain the calculation by using equations, rectangular arrays, and/ or area models.

In this section are the following division strategy worksheets:

Equal Shares

Beth has 15 cupcakes to share with 5 friends.
How many will each friend receive?

15 ÷ 5 =

To make 15, I need: 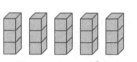 or

5 groups of 3   3 groups of 5

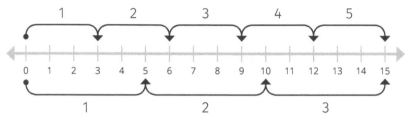

Thus, 15 ÷ 5 = 3

Break the number into equal shares to find possible dividends. You can visualize this using manipulatives or a number line.

Tip: The use of manipulatives is ideal for the struggling learner.

QUESTIONS

• Can you explain how this makes sense?   • Does using a manipulative or number line help?

Estimate first and be prepared to share your thinking.

Paul paid 24 cents for 6 pencils. How much did each pencil cost?	Each drinking glass only holds 3 ounces of apple cider. If there are 24 ounces in the jug of cider, how many drinking glasses will it fill?
The school bus can hold 21 students. If 3 students can sit in each row, how many rows are there?	Mary had 18 hits during 9 recent baseball games. If she had the same number of hits in each game, how many hits did she have in one game?

Repeated Subtraction

What is 54 ÷ 9?

How many nines can be subtracted from 54?

54 − 9 = 45   **1**
45 − 9 = 36   **2**
36 − 9 = 27   **3**
27 − 9 = 18   **4**
18 − 9 = 9   **5**
 9 − 9 = 0   **6**

Therefore, 54 ÷ 9 = 6

You can find out how many nines are in 54 by subtracting 9 until you reach 0. Using this method, you learn that there are 6 nines in 54.

Tip: This strategy works fine for 3rd grade, but becomes unsustainable in 4th grade when you are dividing a 4-digit dividend by a 1-digit divisor, and in 5th grade, when you divide a 4-digit dividend by a 2-digit divisor.

QUESTIONS

- Is repeated subtraction an efficient strategy? Why or why not?
- What do you notice in this pattern of repeated subtraction?

Estimate first and be prepared to share your thinking.

36 ÷ 4	60 ÷ 5	81 ÷ 9
64 ÷ 8	84 ÷ 7	45 ÷ 9
35 ÷ 5	42 ÷ 7	88 ÷ 8

Using an Array

EXAMPLE Mrs. Smith purchased 13 pencils to share with her 2 children. How many pencils will each child get?

$$13 \div 2 =$$

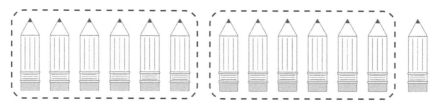

Thus, 13 ÷ 2 = 6 (with 1 left over)

You can visualize this using an array. Each child will get 6 pencils, with 1 left over.

Tip: For struggling learners, start with repeated subtraction, or use a number that can be divided into equal shares without a remainder.

QUESTIONS

- Do you agree with the strategy?
- Do you have another strategy that works?
- Can you explain your strategy?

Estimate first and be prepared to share your thinking.

Bo has 46 baseballs. He has 5 boxes and wants to put the same number of baseballs into each box. How many baseballs will be in each box?	Mr. Howard is taking 71 students on a field trip. He ordered 2 buses. If he wants to balance out the number on each bus, how many students will each bus hold?
There are 74 slots available for 9 students to participate in a tournament. If each student gets the same number of slots, how many slots will each student get?	Meredith needs 27 apples to bake 4 pies. If each pie uses the same number of apples, how many apples will be in each pie?

Relationship Between Multiplication and Division

What is 42 ÷ 7?

Commutative Property

6 groups of 7 is 42

7 groups of 6 is 42

Related Facts

42 ÷ 7 = 6   42 ÷ 6 = 7

6 × 7 = 42   7 × 6 = 42

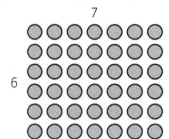

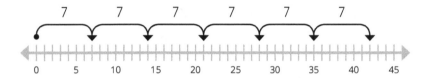

To visually see how 42 objects can be equally divided by 7, you can use an array or a number line. Each of the 7 groups will have exactly 6 objects. Thus, 6 × 7 is 42, and 42 ÷ 7 is 6.

Tip: For struggling learners, use manipulatives or a number line to visualize the problem.

QUESTIONS

- What is the relationship between multiplication and division?
- What are the related facts in this problem?

- Can you explain your strategy using a number line or with color counters?

Estimate first and be prepared to share your thinking.

Kathy has 45 football players to place on 5 different teams. How many players will be on each team?	Derek's classroom vocabulary wall will hold 24 word cards if they are placed in rows of 8. How many rows will be needed to hold all 24 word cards?	A drinking glass holds 8 ounces of juice. If a jug of juice holds 48 ounces of juice, how many drinking glasses can the jug of juice fill?

Using a Number Line

What is 42 ÷ 7?

The number line shows that there are 6 groups of 7 in 42. Subtract 7 from 42 six times to get to 0.

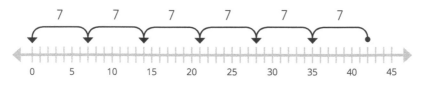

Thus, 42 ÷ 7 = 6

You can use a number line to show that 6 groups of 7 will be 42. Beginning at 0, divide the number line into jumps of 7 until you reach 42. It will take 6 jumps of 7 to get to 42. So, 42 divided into 7 will give you 6.

Tip: Have students verbalize their reasoning and explain their solutions.

QUESTIONS

- How does a number line help you divide?
- Are there limitations with this strategy?
- How is this like another strategy you know?

Estimate first and be prepared to share your thinking.

63 ÷ 9	15 ÷ 3	24 ÷ 4
18 ÷ 6	28 ÷ 7	50 ÷ 10
25 ÷ 5	72 ÷ 9	21 ÷ 7
45 ÷ 5	36 ÷ 4	56 ÷ 7

Tape Diagrams (Strip Diagrams)

EXAMPLE

Beth has 30 markers. Beth has 5 times as many markers as Alice. How many markers does Alice have?

Solve:

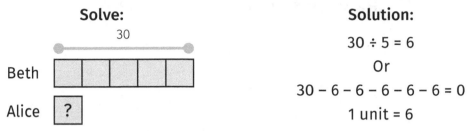

Solution:

$30 \div 5 = 6$

Or

$30 - 6 - 6 - 6 - 6 - 6 = 0$

1 unit = 6

Thus, 30 ÷ 5 = 6

The goal is to find out how many markers Alice has. You know that Beth has 30 markers and that 30 is 5 times as many markers as Alice has. Using a tape diagram, you can visualize how many markers Beth and Alice have to figure out the answer.

Tip: Revoice (repeat back) a student strategy that was shared to make sure you and the other students understand their method of solving the problem.

QUESTIONS

- What information did you need to solve this problem?
- What would be your estimate to the solution?
- Would a manipulative help you solve this problem?
- Is there another strategy you could use to find an answer?

Estimate first and be prepared to share your thinking.

Ms. Smith has 24 students in her math class. If she wants to arrange them in 6 groups, how many students will be in each group?	24
Bill and Steve's frogs raced in a local frog jumping race. Bill's frog jumped 175 inches. Bill's frog jumped 7 times as far as Steve's frog. How far did Steve's frog jump?	175 Bill Steve

Halving

What is 288 ÷ 24?

Halve both numbers: 144 ÷ 12

Halve both again: 72 ÷ 6

Halve both again: 36 ÷ 3

36 ÷ 3 = 12

Thus, 288 ÷ 24 = 12

You can halve each number until you find numbers that are easier to divide.

Tip: A number talk is about productive struggle and the ability to justify, clarify, and discuss mathematics.

QUESTIONS

- Can you restate this strategy?
- How can this problem be solved differently?

Estimate first and be prepared to share your thinking.

96 ÷ 16	52 ÷ 4	72 ÷ 24
140 ÷ 50	500 ÷ 25	184 ÷ 8
144 ÷ 16	168 ÷ 24	392 ÷ 56
112 ÷ 16	192 ÷ 24	176 ÷ 16

Doubling

What is 70 ÷ 35?

Double both numbers: 140 ÷ 70

Now you have numbers that are easier to divide.

140 ÷ 70 = 2

Thus, 70 ÷ 35 = 2

Sometimes, you can double both numbers to make division easier.

Tip: Students should be rephrasing, discussing, critiquing, analyzing, and reflecting during a number talk.

QUESTIONS

- Is this similar to halving? How?
- What is your estimate?
- Why does doubling work?

Estimate first and be prepared to share your thinking.

90 ÷ 45	105 ÷ 35	275 ÷ 25
175 ÷ 35	120 ÷ 15	425 ÷ 25
135 ÷ 45	325 ÷ 25	180 ÷ 45
245 ÷ 35	165 ÷ 15	325 ÷ 25
392 ÷ 7	1,008 ÷ 56	351 ÷ 13

Area Model with 1-Digit Divisors

EXAMPLE

What is 108 ÷ 9?

(90 + 9 + 9)

10 + 1 + 1 = 12

90	9	9

9

Thus, 108 ÷ 9 = 12

Decompose the dividend, 108, into easier multiples of 9 (90 + 9 + 9). Divide these decomposed numbers by the divisor, 9. Then add up the results to find the quotient. The quotient is 10 + 1 + 1, or 12.

Tip: Begin with smaller numbers so all students, even struggling students, have an entry point to solving the problem.

QUESTIONS

• How are the dividend, divisor, and quotient related in an area model?

• How is this similar to using an area model for multiplication?

• What would happen if you have a remainder?

Estimate first and be prepared to share your thinking.

45 ÷ 3	64 ÷ 4	72 ÷ 8
120 ÷ 8	304 ÷ 4	192 ÷ 6
182 ÷ 7	528 ÷ 8	756 ÷ 9

Area Model with 2-Digit Divisors

What is 330 ÷ 15?

(100 + 100 + 50 + 50 + 20 + 10)

×	10 + 10 + 2 = 22		
10 +	100	100	20
5	50	50	10

Thus, 330 ÷ 15 = 22

First, decompose the divisor (15) into 10 + 5 to make it easier to multiply. Then, multiply 10 and 5 by the landmark number 10 to get 100 and 50 (150), then by 10 again to get 100 and 50 (150), then by 2 to get 20 and 10 (30). The area of the rectangle is now 330, the dividend. Add the partial products 10, 10, and 2 together to find the quotient, 22.

Tip: Use student errors to explore other strategies that will work.

QUESTIONS

- How are the dividend, divisor, and quotient related in an area model?
- How is this similar to using an area model for multiplication?
- What would happen if you have a remainder?

Estimate first and be prepared to share your thinking.

375 ÷ 15	240 ÷ 16	918 ÷ 34
294 ÷ 21	800 ÷ 25	782 ÷ 23
782 ÷ 17	812 ÷ 14	572 ÷ 22

Decomposition and Distributed Division

What is 624 ÷ 4?

Decompose 624 to 400 + 200 + 24

(400 ÷ 4) + (200 ÷ 4) + (24 ÷ 4)

⌄   ⌄   ⌄

100   +   50   +   6   = 156

Thus, 624 ÷ 4 = 156

Decompose the dividend 624 into easier numbers that can be quickly divided by 4.

Tip: Ask students to estimate the solution before sharing strategies.

QUESTIONS

- Would it matter what number is used when decomposing the dividend?
- Can you prove this strategy works?
- Is this an efficient strategy?

Estimate first and be prepared to share your thinking.

232 ÷ 4	525 ÷ 5	847 ÷ 7
960 ÷ 3	954 ÷ 9	546 ÷ 6
4,848 ÷ 4	5,450 ÷ 5	104 ÷ 8
245 ÷ 5	264 ÷ 3	3,846 ÷ 3
1,568 ÷ 7	5,450 ÷ 5	6,328 ÷ 2

Partial Quotients with Smaller Numbers

What is 84 ÷ 3?

```
3 | 84   10
    30
    54   10
    30
    24    4
    12
    12    4
    12
```

10 + 10 + 4 + 4 = 28

You can multiply the divisor by landmark numbers, like tens, and then subtract the product from the dividend to make dividing easy. Then you can multiply by smaller numbers and subtract those products from the dividend, too. Instead of multiplying by 4 two times at the end of the problem, you could have multiplied by 8, twos, or ones. Once you've subtracted down to zero, you can add up all the numbers you multiplied by to find the quotient.

Thus, 84 ÷ 3 = 28

Tip: With division, you might think about letting students jot down their thinking. Mental math with division is difficult when the numbers get larger.

QUESTIONS

- Are there limitations with this strategy?
- Can you explain this strategy in your own words?
- What patterns do you notice?
- What would this look like if you had used an 8, 2, or 1 to multiply by?

Estimate first and be prepared to share your thinking.

96 ÷ 8	92 ÷ 4	88 ÷ 4
78 ÷ 3	91 ÷ 7	95 ÷ 5
92 ÷ 7	89 ÷ 4	80 ÷ 6

Partial Quotients with Larger Numbers

What is 504 ÷ 12?

```
12 │ 504 │ 10
    │ 120 │
    │ 384 │ 10
    │ 120 │
    │ 264 │ 10
    │ 120 │
    │ 144 │ 10
    │ 120 │
    │  24 │ 2
    │  24 │
```

10 + 10 + 10 + 10 + 2 = 42

Thus, 504 ÷ 12 = 42

Tip: Use numbers all students can be successful with.

QUESTIONS

• Is this like another strategy you know?   • Why does this work?

Estimate first and be prepared to share your thinking.

125 ÷ 5	184 ÷ 8	621 ÷ 27
902 ÷ 22	720 ÷ 40	325 ÷ 13
832 ÷ 26	273 ÷ 17	833 ÷ 32

Place Value Columns
(1-digit divisor/2-digit dividend)

What is 84 ÷ 7?

```
      1 2
   7 | 8   4
     -7    14
      1    -14
            0
```

$$84 ÷ 7 = 12$$

Separate the dividend into place value columns and divide first the tens and then the ones by 7. After subtracting the tens (80 - 70), the leftover group of 10 was added to the 4 ones.

Tip: The art of explaining thinking is more important than arriving at an answer.

QUESTIONS

• What would happen if you had a remainder?

• How would you explain your thinking?

• Can you prove this strategy works?

Estimate first and be prepared to share your thinking.

54 ÷ 6	60 ÷ 5	81 ÷ 9
42 ÷ 7	56 ÷ 8	72 ÷ 6
35 ÷ 5	48 ÷ 6	32 ÷ 8

Place Value Columns
(1-digit divisor/3-digit dividend)

What is 642 ÷ 6?

```
    1 0  7
6 | 6 4  2
   -6   ↘42
    0   -42
         0
```

642 ÷ 6 = 107

Separate the dividend into place value columns and divide the hundreds, tens, and ones columns by 6. Add 4 tens to the 2 ones to make 42.

Tip: You might consider allowing paper and pencil for the thinking process.

QUESTIONS

- Do you agree with the strategy given? Can you state it in your own words?
- What would happen if there were a remainder?

Estimate first and be prepared to share your thinking.

168 ÷ 3	568 ÷ 4	565 ÷ 5
738 ÷ 6	686 ÷ 7	928 ÷ 8
674 ÷ 9	306 ÷ 3	684 ÷ 6
736 ÷ 8	655 ÷ 5	884 ÷ 4

Place Value Columns
(1-digit divisor/4-digit dividend)

What is 5,075 ÷ 5?

```
        1 0 1  5
   5  | 5 0 7  5
       -5  -5
        0   2  25
               -25
                 0
```

5,075 ÷ 5 = 1,015

Separate the dividend into place value columns and divide the thousands, hundreds, tens, and ones by 5. Add 2 tens to the 5 ones to make 25.

Tip: You might consider allowing paper and pencil for the thinking process.

QUESTIONS

- What estimate did you get?
- Do you have a strategy you want to share?
- Is there another strategy that was similar to this?

Estimate first and be prepared to share your thinking.

7,718 ÷ 2	1,008 ÷ 4	6,075 ÷ 5
2,136 ÷ 6	2,513 ÷ 7	2,424 ÷ 8
1,404 ÷ 9	9,691 ÷ 3	3,144 ÷ 6
3,616 ÷ 8	1,720 ÷ 5	2,484 ÷ 4

Finding the Missing Side of a Rectangle

Paul and Ally are designing a large garden for their grandmother. If they want the area of the garden to be 180 yards with a length of 12 yards, what will the width be?

You know the following: Area = length × width.

$$180 = 12 \times ?$$
$$180 \div 12 = ?$$
$$180 \div 12 = 15$$

| A = 180 yards | 12 yards |

The width is 15 yards

Area is the number of square units needed to cover a region, and a rectangle is an array of square units. The garden covers 180 square yards and has a length of 12 yards. The missing side width can be found by dividing 180 square yards into multiple columns of 12 yards.

Tip: For struggling learners, use manipulatives such as color tiles or geoboards/geoboard paper to find the missing side of a rectangle.

QUESTIONS

- What strategy that you already know will help you solve for the missing length or width?
- How does knowing your fact families help you with area problems?

- Would knowing perimeter help solve for area?
- What strategy can you use to find a solution?

Estimate first and be prepared to share your thinking.

Find the missing width of the front of the fish tank, which has an area of 768 in².	Find the missing length of the iPad, which has an area of 63 in².	Find the missing width of the top of the desk, which has an area of 570 in².
 ? in 48 in	? in 7 in	? in 19 in

Common Multiplication and Division Situations

	Unknown Product	Group Size Unknown ("How Many In Each Group?" Division)	Number Of Groups Unknown ("How Many Groups?" Division)
	3 x 6 = ?	3 x ? = 18, and 18 ÷ 3 = ?	? x 6 = 18, and 18 ÷ 6 = ?
Equal Groups	There are 3 bags with 6 plums in each bag. How many plums are there in all? You need 3 lengths of string, each 6 inches long. How much string will you need altogether?	If 18 plums are shared equally into 3 bags, then how many plums will be in each bag? You have 18 inches of string, which you will cut into 3 equal pieces. How long will each piece of string be?	If 18 plums are to be packed 6 to a bag, then how many bags are needed? You have 18 inches of string, which you will cut into pieces that are 6 inches long. How many pieces of string will you have?
Arrays, Area	There are 3 rows of apples with 6 apples in each row. How many apples are there? What is the area of a 3 cm by 6 cm rectangle?	If 18 apples are arranged into 3 equal rows, how many apples will be in each row? A rectangle has an area of 18 square centimeters. If one side is 3 cm long, how long is a side next to it?	If 18 apples are arranged into equal rows of 6 apples, how many rows will there be? A rectangle has area 18 square centimeters. If one side is 6 cm long, how long is a side next to it?
Compare	A blue hat costs $6. A red hat costs 3 times as much as the blue hat. How much does the red hat cost? A rubber band is 6 cm long. How long will the rubber band be when it is stretched to be 3 times as long?	A red hat costs $18 and that is 3 times as much as a blue hat costs. How much does a blue hat cost? A rubber band is stretched to be 18 cm long and that is 3 times as long as it was at first. How long was the rubber band at first?	A red hat costs $18 and a blue hat costs $6. How many times as much does the red hat cost as the blue hat? A rubber band was 6 cm long at first. Now it is stretched to be 18 cm long. How many times as long is the rubber band now as it was at first?
General	a x b = ?	a x ? = p and p ÷ a = ?	? x b = p, and p ÷ b = ?

Fractions

"Fractions are a critical foundation for students, as they are used in measurement across various professions, and they are essential to the study of algebra and more advanced mathematics."

—*John A. Van de Walle*

4.NF.B.3.A Understand addition and subtraction of fractions as joining and separating parts referring to the same whole.

4.NF.B.3.C Add and subtract mixed numbers with like denominators.

5.NF.A.1 Add and subtract fractions with unlike denominators (including mixed numbers) by replacing given fractions with equivalent fractions in such a way as to produce an equivalent sum or difference of fractions with like denominators.

5.NF.B.4 Apply and extend previous understandings of multiplication to multiply a fraction or whole number by a fraction.

5.NF.B.4.B Find the area of a rectangle with fractional side lengths by tiling it with unit squares of the appropriate unit fraction side lengths, and show that the area is the same as would be found by multiplying the side lengths. Multiply fractional side lengths to find areas of rectangles, and represent fraction products as rectangular areas.

5.NF.B.7 Apply and extend previous understandings of division to divide unit fractions by whole numbers and whole numbers by unit fractions.

In this section are the following fraction strategy worksheets:

Fraction Fundamentals

Addition

Subtraction

Fair Shares and Partitioning

How can you equally share 4 sub sandwiches with 6 people?

| 1 | 1 | 2 | 2 | 3 | 3 | 4 | 4 | 5 | 5 | 6 | 6 |

The strategy is to divide each sub into 3 equal parts. Now you can equally share the subs so each person gets 2 parts.

Tip: Number talks are based on numerical relationships to teach adding, subtracting, multiplying, and dividing.

QUESTIONS

- What strategy did you use?
- Can you explain your reasoning?

- How does this work?
- Can you show this with a manipulative?

How can you equally share 4 pies with 3 friends?	How many fourths are in $\frac{5}{8}$?	What is half of $\frac{1}{4}$?
What fraction is shown? 0 ———•— 1	Where is $\frac{3}{8}$ located on this number line? 0 —————— 1	Where would $\frac{2}{3}$ be located on this number line? 0 —————— 1

Fractions 101

Set Models

If 8 counters are a whole set,
how many are in $\frac{1}{4}$ of a set?

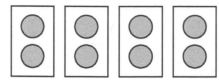

There are 8 counters total. If you partition the set into groups of 4, you'll find that there are 2 counters in $\frac{1}{4}$ of a set.

Tip: Students understand that numbers are composed of smaller numbers that can be composed and decomposed to make new numbers.

QUESTIONS

- What does the denominator tell you?
- What does the numerator tell you?

- Can you describe a set that describes the fraction?
- Where would you place this fraction on a number line?

If 15 counters are in a whole set, how many counters make $\frac{3}{5}$ of the set?	If 12 counters are $\frac{3}{4}$ of a set, how many counters are in the full set?
If 10 counters are 5 halves of a set, how many counters are in one set?	If 2 counters are $\frac{1}{5}$ of a set, how many counters are in the full set?

More, Less, or Equal to One Whole

Will the fractions shown below make a number that is greater, less than, or equal to one whole?

It will be greater than one whole because 3 thirds will make one whole.

Tip: For struggling learners, have fraction tiles, fraction strips, or fraction circles available.

QUESTIONS

- How do you know it is greater, less than, or equal to a whole?
- Can you use a number line to show this?

- Can you use fraction tiles to explain your reasoning?
- How do you know that 3 thirds make a whole?

Estimate first and be prepared to share your thinking.

Will the fractions shown below make a number that is greater, less than, or equal to one whole?

Will the fractions shown below make a number that is greater, less than, or equal to one whole?

Will the fractions shown below make a number that is greater, less than, or equal to one whole?

Comparing Fractions

Which fraction is greater?

$$\frac{2}{3} \quad \text{or} \quad \frac{3}{4}$$

1											
$\frac{1}{2}$						$\frac{1}{2}$					
$\frac{1}{3}$				$\frac{1}{3}$				$\frac{1}{3}$			
$\frac{1}{4}$			$\frac{1}{4}$			$\frac{1}{4}$			$\frac{1}{4}$		
$\frac{1}{5}$		$\frac{1}{5}$		$\frac{1}{5}$		$\frac{1}{5}$			$\frac{1}{5}$		
$\frac{1}{6}$		$\frac{1}{6}$		$\frac{1}{6}$		$\frac{1}{6}$		$\frac{1}{6}$		$\frac{1}{6}$	
$\frac{1}{8}$	$\frac{1}{8}$	$\frac{1}{8}$	$\frac{1}{8}$	$\frac{1}{8}$	$\frac{1}{8}$	$\frac{1}{8}$	$\frac{1}{8}$				
$\frac{1}{10}$	$\frac{1}{10}$	$\frac{1}{10}$	$\frac{1}{10}$	$\frac{1}{10}$	$\frac{1}{10}$	$\frac{1}{10}$	$\frac{1}{10}$	$\frac{1}{10}$	$\frac{1}{10}$		
$\frac{1}{12}$	$\frac{1}{12}$	$\frac{1}{12}$	$\frac{1}{12}$	$\frac{1}{12}$	$\frac{1}{12}$	$\frac{1}{12}$	$\frac{1}{12}$	$\frac{1}{12}$	$\frac{1}{12}$	$\frac{1}{12}$	$\frac{1}{12}$

You know that $\frac{3}{4}$ is greater than $\frac{2}{3}$ because when you compare with fraction tiles, $\frac{3}{4}$ is longer.

Tip: Have students share their strategies.

QUESTIONS

- How does this compare to using a number line? Which is more effective?

- Does the use of fraction tiles help you see the relationship between the fractions?

- Can you compare the 2 fractions using another strategy?

Which fraction is greater?

$\frac{5}{10}$ or $\frac{1}{2}$	$\frac{5}{6}$ or $\frac{8}{12}$	$\frac{3}{6}$ or $\frac{1}{12}$
$\frac{5}{6}$ or $\frac{7}{8}$	$\frac{5}{9}$ or $\frac{1}{2}$	$\frac{3}{10}$ or $\frac{5}{7}$

Ordering Fractions

Order the fractions from least to greatest.

$$\frac{1}{9}, \frac{1}{3}, \frac{1}{2}, \frac{1}{8}$$

1											

A fraction tiles chart showing 1 whole, halves, thirds, fourths, fifths, sixths, eighths, tenths, and twelfths.

You can compare and order the fractions using fraction tiles. You can also use your understanding of the denominator to determine the order: $\frac{1}{9}, \frac{1}{8}, \frac{1}{3}, \frac{1}{2}$.

Tip: It is important for students to explain their thinking and share with the class.

QUESTIONS

- How do fraction tiles help you order fractions?
- How does knowing the meaning of the numerator and denominator help you order fractions?

- Which fraction is the largest? Explain.
- Which fraction is the smallest? Explain.

Order the following fractions from least to greatest

$\frac{3}{12}, \frac{1}{5}, \frac{1}{2}, \frac{5}{6}$	$\frac{4}{8}, \frac{2}{6}, \frac{2}{12}, \frac{3}{4}$
$\frac{5}{8}, \frac{2}{5}, \frac{1}{12}, \frac{3}{4}$	$\frac{2}{3}, \frac{3}{10}, \frac{4}{5}, \frac{1}{8}$
$\frac{3}{10}, \frac{3}{8}, \frac{3}{5}, \frac{3}{6}$	$\frac{3}{4}, \frac{9}{10}, \frac{4}{5}, \frac{5}{6}$

Equivalent Fractions Using Fraction Tiles

EXAMPLE ### What fractions are equivalent $\frac{1}{2}$?

1											
$\frac{1}{2}$						$\frac{1}{2}$					
$\frac{1}{3}$			$\frac{1}{3}$			$\frac{1}{3}$					
$\frac{1}{4}$		$\frac{1}{4}$		$\frac{1}{4}$			$\frac{1}{4}$				
$\frac{1}{5}$		$\frac{1}{5}$		$\frac{1}{5}$		$\frac{1}{5}$		$\frac{1}{5}$			
$\frac{1}{6}$		$\frac{1}{6}$		$\frac{1}{6}$		$\frac{1}{6}$		$\frac{1}{6}$		$\frac{1}{6}$	
$\frac{1}{8}$	$\frac{1}{8}$	$\frac{1}{8}$	$\frac{1}{8}$	$\frac{1}{8}$	$\frac{1}{8}$	$\frac{1}{8}$	$\frac{1}{8}$				
$\frac{1}{10}$	$\frac{1}{10}$	$\frac{1}{10}$	$\frac{1}{10}$	$\frac{1}{10}$	$\frac{1}{10}$	$\frac{1}{10}$	$\frac{1}{10}$	$\frac{1}{10}$	$\frac{1}{10}$		
$\frac{1}{12}$	$\frac{1}{12}$	$\frac{1}{12}$	$\frac{1}{12}$	$\frac{1}{12}$	$\frac{1}{12}$	$\frac{1}{12}$	$\frac{1}{12}$	$\frac{1}{12}$	$\frac{1}{12}$	$\frac{1}{12}$	$\frac{1}{12}$

You can determine equivalency by using fraction tiles. $\frac{2}{4}$, $\frac{3}{6}$, $\frac{4}{8}$, $\frac{5}{10}$, and $\frac{6}{12}$ are examples of equivalent fractions—they all represent the same amount.

Tip: For students with understanding, remove the fraction tiles or other manipulatives you are using.

QUESTIONS

- How do fraction tiles help you see equivalency?
- What does equivalency mean?
- Is there another way to determine equivalency?
- What strategy did you use?

Which fraction is equivalent to...?

$\frac{4}{12}$	$\frac{2}{6}$	$\frac{1}{4}$
$\frac{6}{8}$	$\frac{3}{15}$	$\frac{3}{5}$
$\frac{1}{3}$	$\frac{8}{10}$	$\frac{1}{2}$

Equivalent Fractions Using a Number Line

Is $\frac{6}{8}$ equivalent to $\frac{3}{4}$?

$$\frac{6}{8} = \frac{3}{4}$$

You can divide a number line into 8 equal parts and another number line into 4 equal parts. Once you shade in $\frac{6}{8}$ and $\frac{3}{4}$, you can see they are equivalent.

Tip: Make sure all students are participating and listening respectfully.

QUESTIONS

- How can you tell the fractions are equivalent?
- What does equivalency mean?

- What part of the number line do you shade in for both fractions?
- How do you know how many parts to divide the number line into?

Are these fractions equivalent?

$\frac{2}{3}$ and $\frac{3}{4}$	$\frac{1}{5}$ and $\frac{3}{15}$	$\frac{8}{12}$ and $\frac{1}{2}$
$\frac{4}{12}$ and $\frac{1}{3}$	$\frac{8}{10}$ and $\frac{3}{5}$	$\frac{6}{12}$ and $\frac{3}{4}$
$\frac{4}{5}$ and $\frac{6}{10}$	$\frac{3}{7}$ and $\frac{6}{10}$	$\frac{7}{8}$ and $\frac{8}{9}$

Decomposing Fractions

Decompose $\frac{5}{8}$.

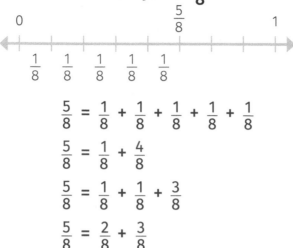

$$\frac{5}{8} = \frac{1}{8} + \frac{1}{8} + \frac{1}{8} + \frac{1}{8} + \frac{1}{8}$$

$$\frac{5}{8} = \frac{1}{8} + \frac{4}{8}$$

$$\frac{5}{8} = \frac{1}{8} + \frac{1}{8} + \frac{3}{8}$$

$$\frac{5}{8} = \frac{2}{8} + \frac{3}{8}$$

If you make 5 copies of $\frac{1}{8}$, you get $\frac{5}{8}$. Remember that unit fractions are the basic building blocks of fractions and will help when computing and understanding fractions.

Tip: Have students discuss possible solutions prior to sharing.

QUESTIONS

- How did you decompose this fraction?
- Why is it important to understand unit fractions?

- How does decomposing fractions help you understand the fraction?
- What combination did you have? Is there another combination that will work?

How many different ways can you think of to decompose this fraction?

$\frac{4}{12}$	$\frac{3}{4}$	$\frac{5}{8}$
$\frac{7}{8}$	$\frac{3}{5}$	$\frac{5}{6}$

Decomposing Fractions Using Tape Diagrams and Number Bonds

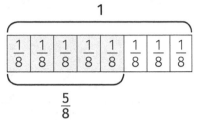

EXAMPLE

Decompose $\frac{5}{8}$.

1

| $\frac{1}{8}$ | $\frac{1}{8}$ | $\frac{1}{8}$ | $\frac{1}{8}$ | $\frac{1}{8}$ | $\frac{1}{8}$ | $\frac{1}{8}$ | $\frac{1}{8}$ |

$\frac{5}{8}$

Example addition sentences and number bond:

$$\frac{5}{8} = \frac{3}{8} + \frac{2}{8}$$

$$\frac{5}{8} = \frac{4}{8} + \frac{1}{8}$$

If you make 5 copies of $\frac{1}{8}$, you get $\frac{5}{8}$. You can write an addition sentence that will decompose $\frac{5}{8}$ several different ways.

Tip: Provide enough wait time so all students have time to come up with a solution.

QUESTIONS

- How does decomposing fractions help you understand them?

- What is the missing fraction in this number bond... $\frac{5}{8}$, $\frac{1}{2}$, _____?

- What would your number bond look like if $\frac{5}{8}$ was the whole and $\frac{1}{4}$ was one of the parts?

What number sentence will you use on the number bond?

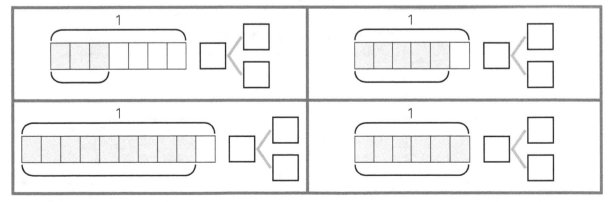

Adding Fractions Using Fraction Tiles

EXAMPLE

$$\frac{2}{3} + \frac{2}{9} = ?$$

$$\frac{6}{9} + \frac{2}{9} = \frac{8}{9}$$

You cannot add these fractions without a common denominator. You can partition $\frac{2}{3}$ into 9 parts to match $\frac{2}{9}$ and rename $\frac{2}{3}$ as $\frac{6}{9}$. Now you can add these fractions with a common denominator.

Tip: Make sure students share their thinking and avoid procedural responses. Conceptual understanding is the key to a number talk.

QUESTIONS

- How can you use fraction tiles to add fractions?
- What do you need to change to make it possible to add the fractions?
- Which fraction needs to be renamed?
- Do you need to rename both fractions?

Add the fractions using fraction tiles.

$\frac{5}{8} + \frac{1}{2}$	$\frac{1}{2} + \frac{1}{4}$	$\frac{2}{5} + \frac{3}{10}$
$\frac{2}{4} + \frac{2}{3}$	$\frac{3}{6} + \frac{1}{3}$	$\frac{2}{8} + \frac{3}{4}$

Adding Fractions Using a Number Line: Like Denominators

$$\frac{3}{8} + \frac{2}{8} = \frac{5}{8}$$

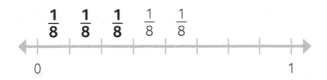

Adding fractions with like denominators on a number line is easy. Since the denominator is 8, you can divide the number line into 8 segments. Then, add $\frac{3}{8}$ with $\frac{2}{8}$ and get $\frac{5}{8}$.

Tip: For struggling students, make sure students can decompose fractions into unit fractions.

QUESTIONS

- Can you use fraction tiles to show addition of fractions?
- What do you notice about the numerators and denominators?

Add the fractions using a number line.

$\frac{5}{9} + \frac{2}{9}$	$\frac{1}{2} + \frac{1}{2}$	$\frac{2}{7} + \frac{3}{7}$
$\frac{2}{4} + \frac{1}{4}$	$\frac{3}{6} + \frac{1}{6}$	$\frac{2}{8} + \frac{3}{8}$
$\frac{2}{5} + \frac{3}{5}$	$\frac{1}{3} + \frac{1}{3}$	$\frac{3}{9} + \frac{5}{9}$
$\frac{3}{4} + \frac{3}{4}$	$\frac{2}{6} + \frac{4}{6}$	$\frac{4}{8} + \frac{7}{8}$

Adding Fractions Using a Number Line: Unlike Denominators

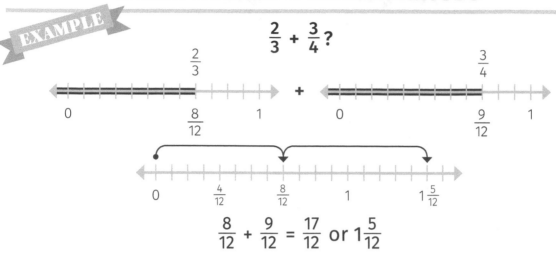

$$\frac{8}{12} + \frac{9}{12} = \frac{17}{12} \text{ or } 1\frac{5}{12}$$

You cannot add thirds and fourths because they have different denominators. You need to find an equivalent fraction for both $\frac{2}{3}$ and $\frac{3}{4}$. Rename $\frac{2}{3}$ to the equivalent fraction $\frac{8}{12}$, and $\frac{3}{4}$ to the equivalent fraction $\frac{9}{12}$. Now their denominators are the same, and you can add.

Tip: For struggling students, step back to adding with like denominators.

QUESTIONS

- Is it possible to add $\frac{2}{3}$ and $\frac{3}{4}$?
- How does a number line help you add fractions with unlike denominators?

- How can you change thirds and fourths so they can be added?
- How is this alike or different from adding on a number line with like denominators?

Add the fractions using a number line.

$\frac{1}{9} + \frac{2}{3}$	$\frac{1}{2} + \frac{2}{6}$	$\frac{2}{7} + \frac{1}{2}$
$\frac{3}{8} + \frac{1}{4}$	$\frac{2}{3} + \frac{5}{6}$	$\frac{3}{8} + \frac{3}{4}$
$\frac{2}{5} + \frac{3}{10}$	$\frac{1}{3} + \frac{1}{6}$	$\frac{1}{9} + \frac{5}{6}$

Adding Fractions Using a Tape Diagram: Like Denominators

EXAMPLE

What is $\frac{3}{5} + \frac{4}{5}$?

$$\frac{3}{5} + \frac{4}{5} = \frac{7}{5} \text{ or } 1\frac{2}{5}$$

Since the denominator is 5, you know that there are five fifths in a whole. Using the tape diagram, you can see that the answer is more than 1 whole.

Tip: For struggling learners, use manipulatives such as fraction tiles or fraction circles.

QUESTIONS

- How do you know how many parts to divide the diagram into?
- Why does the sum equal a number greater than 1?
- How did you rename 7/5?
- How would you add these numbers using fraction tiles?

Add the fractions using a tape diagram.

$\frac{5}{6} + \frac{3}{6}$	$\frac{1}{4} + \frac{2}{4}$	$\frac{3}{7} + \frac{5}{7}$
$\frac{2}{8} + \frac{5}{8}$	$\frac{5}{9} + \frac{5}{9}$	$\frac{2}{6} + \frac{5}{6}$
$\frac{2}{5} + \frac{3}{5}$	$\frac{4}{7} + \frac{6}{7}$	$\frac{4}{5} + \frac{4}{5}$
$\frac{3}{4} + \frac{2}{4}$	$\frac{6}{8} + \frac{3}{8}$	$\frac{1}{4} + \frac{3}{4}$

Adding Fractions Using an Area Model: Unlike Denominators

EXAMPLE

What is $\frac{2}{3} + \frac{3}{5}$?

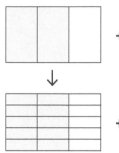 +

Shaded parts represent the numerator. Total parts represent the denominator.

↓   ↓

+

Rename the fractions with common denominator.

$\frac{2}{3}$ is renamed to $\frac{10}{15}$, with 10 shaded parts out of a total of 15.

$\frac{3}{5}$ is renamed to $\frac{9}{15}$, with 9 shaded parts out of a total of 15.

$$\frac{10}{15} + \frac{9}{15} = \frac{19}{15} \ or \ 1\frac{4}{15}$$

In order to add these two fractions, they must have the same denominator. Begin by making an area model of each fraction. Combine the models by placing the $\frac{2}{3}$ over the $\frac{3}{5}$ and the $\frac{3}{5}$ over the $\frac{2}{3}$, which divides both shapes into 15 parts. This shows that 15 is a common denominator. Now you can add.

Tip: For struggling students, step back to adding with like denominators.

QUESTIONS

- Why can't you add $\frac{2}{3}$ and $\frac{3}{5}$ with current denominators?
- Why must they have the same denominator?
- Why must you rename the fractions?
- How can you partition thirds and fifths so they are equal?

Add the fractions using an area model.

$\frac{1}{5} + \frac{2}{3}$	$\frac{1}{2} + \frac{3}{8}$	$\frac{2}{7} + \frac{1}{2}$
$\frac{2}{5} + \frac{1}{4}$	$\frac{2}{3} + \frac{4}{5}$	$\frac{5}{6} + \frac{3}{4}$

Adding Fractions Using Decomposition

EXAMPLE

What is $\frac{3}{4} + \frac{7}{8}$?

$$\frac{1}{4} + \frac{1}{4} + \frac{1}{4} = \frac{1}{8} + \frac{1}{8} + \frac{1}{8} + \frac{1}{8} + \frac{1}{8} + \frac{1}{8}, \text{ or } \frac{6}{8}$$

$$\left(\frac{1}{8} + \frac{1}{8} + \frac{1}{8} + \frac{1}{8} + \frac{1}{8} + \frac{1}{8}\right) + \left(\frac{7}{8}\right) = ?$$

$$\frac{5}{8} + \left(\frac{1}{8} + \frac{7}{8}\right) = \frac{5}{8} + 1 \text{ or } 1\frac{5}{8}$$

Decompose $\frac{3}{4}$ to unit fractions, and then decompose those unit fractions to eighths (each fourth is the same as 2 eighths). Then, add up all the eighths.

Tip: For struggling students, use a number line.

QUESTIONS

- How can you decompose $\frac{3}{4}$ to its unit fractions?
- How can $\frac{1}{4}$ be decomposed to 2 eighths?

- Why combine $\frac{1}{8}$ and $\frac{7}{8}$ to add?
- Can you explain your thinking?

Add the fractions using decomposition.

$\frac{5}{6} + \frac{1}{2}$	$\frac{5}{8} + \frac{1}{2}$
$\frac{5}{6} + \frac{2}{3}$	$\frac{5}{8} + \frac{1}{2}$
$\frac{11}{12} + \frac{4}{6}$	$\frac{3}{4} + \frac{5}{8}$
$\frac{4}{5} + \frac{3}{10}$	$\frac{2}{6} + \frac{2}{3}$

Adding Fractions Using Equivalency

What is $\frac{2}{3} + \frac{1}{8}$?

Equivalent Fractions   Equivalent Fractions

$\frac{4}{6}$ $\frac{6}{9}$ $\frac{8}{12}$ $\frac{1}{4}$ $\frac{10}{15}$ $\frac{12}{18}$ $\frac{14}{21}$ $\boxed{\frac{16}{24}}$ $\frac{2}{16}$ $\boxed{\frac{3}{24}}$ $\frac{4}{32}$ $\frac{5}{40}$

$$\frac{16}{24} + \frac{3}{24} = \frac{19}{24}$$

You can easily add fractions by listing equivalent fractions, then finding the fractions with the same denominators. $\frac{2}{3}$ is equivalent to $\frac{16}{24}$, and $\frac{1}{8}$ is equivalent to $\frac{3}{24}$.

$$\frac{16}{24} + \frac{3}{24} = \frac{19}{24}, \text{ so } \frac{2}{3} + \frac{1}{8} = \frac{19}{24}$$

Tip: For struggling students, step back to adding with like denominators, or using manipulatives such as fraction tiles and fraction circles.

QUESTIONS

- Can you add these fractions without finding a common denominator?

- What strategy can you use?

- Can you share your thinking?

- Can you list equivalent fractions to $\frac{2}{3}$?

- Can you list equivalent fractions to $\frac{1}{8}$?

- What equivalent fractions have the same denominator?

Add the fractions using equivalency.

$\frac{2}{5} + \frac{5}{6}$	$\frac{2}{6} + \frac{3}{4}$	$\frac{2}{7} + \frac{1}{2}$
$\frac{2}{5} + \frac{1}{4}$	$\frac{2}{3} + \frac{4}{5}$	$\frac{5}{6} + \frac{3}{4}$
$\frac{2}{5} + \frac{3}{4}$	$\frac{1}{3} + \frac{1}{5}$	$\frac{2}{7} + \frac{1}{4}$
$\frac{3}{4} + \frac{2}{3}$	$\frac{2}{6} + \frac{1}{5}$	$\frac{1}{2} + \frac{3}{5}$

Adding Fractions Using Tape Diagrams

A cake recipe calls for $\frac{2}{4}$ cup of milk and $\frac{1}{4}$ cup of oil. How much liquid is required to make the cake?

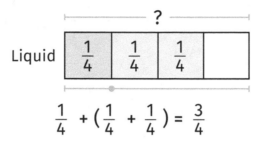

$$\frac{1}{4} + \left(\frac{1}{4} + \frac{1}{4}\right) = \frac{3}{4}$$

Tip: For struggling students, step back to adding with like denominators, or using manipulatives such as fraction tiles and fraction circles.

QUESTIONS

- How does a tape diagram help you solve this problem?
- What information do you have?
- What information is missing?

- What strategy will you use to find your solution?
- Can you share your strategy with another student?

Use tape diagrams to solve the following word problems.

Richard spends $\frac{2}{6}$ of his daily time in school and $\frac{1}{6}$ of his time doing homework. What fraction of his day was spent in school and doing homework?

Richard's Day

Ben and Susan shared a pizza for lunch. Ben ate $\frac{4}{7}$ of the pizza and Susan $\frac{2}{7}$ of the pizza. What fraction of the pizza did they eat?

Total Pizza

Sylvia ate $\frac{5}{12}$ of a box of chocolates. Her sister Joan ate $\frac{1}{12}$ more than Sylvia. What part of the box of chocolate did they eat?

Box of Chocolates

Finding Perimeter by Adding Lengths

What is the perimeter of this shape?

$\frac{5}{6}$ units

$\frac{2}{6}$ units

$$\frac{5}{6} + \frac{5}{6} + \frac{2}{6} + \frac{2}{6} = P$$

$$\frac{14}{6} = P$$

$$2\frac{2}{6} \text{ or } 2\frac{1}{3} \text{ units}$$

Perimeter is the sum of the length of each side. Find the perimeter of this shape by adding all the side lengths.

Tip: For the struggling learner, use a geoboard paper or fraction tiles and have students count the side lengths.

QUESTIONS

- Is this similar to another strategy you know?
- What strategy did you use to add? Explain.

- Will you get the same answer if you add the length and width and then double the answer? Why does this work?

Find the perimeter.

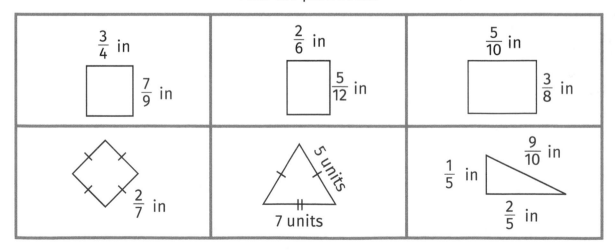

Subtracting Fractions Using Fraction Tiles

EXAMPLE $\frac{7}{10} - \frac{3}{5} = ?$

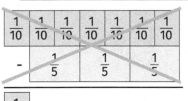

$\frac{6}{10} = \frac{3}{5}$

$\frac{7}{10} - \frac{3}{5} = \frac{1}{10}$

You cannot subtract these fractions without a common denominator. You can see that $\frac{1}{5}$ is the same as $\frac{2}{10}$. Thus, you know that $\frac{3}{5}$ will be the same as $\frac{6}{10}$. Subtracting $\frac{3}{5}$ is the same as subtracting $\frac{6}{10}$.

Tip: For struggling learners, subtract with like denominators or step back to addition of fractions.

QUESTIONS

- How can you use fraction tiles to subtract these fractions?
- Which fraction needs to be renamed?

- Do you need to rename both fractions?
- How do you know that $\frac{2}{10}$ is the same as $\frac{1}{5}$?

Subtract the fractions using fraction tiles.

$\frac{5}{8} - \frac{1}{2}$	$\frac{1}{2} - \frac{1}{4}$	$\frac{2}{5} - \frac{3}{10}$
$\frac{7}{12} - \frac{2}{3}$	$\frac{3}{6} - \frac{1}{3}$	$\frac{7}{8} - \frac{2}{4}$
$\frac{5}{12} - \frac{1}{4}$	$\frac{2}{3} - \frac{2}{12}$	$\frac{3}{4} - \frac{3}{8}$

Subtracting Fractions Using a Number Line: Like Denominators

EXAMPLE

What is $\frac{3}{4} - \frac{1}{4}$?

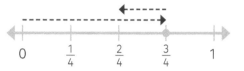

$$\frac{3}{4} - \frac{1}{4} = \frac{2}{4} \text{ or } \frac{1}{2}$$

The denominators are the same, so you can easily subtract. Jump to $\frac{3}{4}$ on a number line, then move back $\frac{1}{4}$ to $\frac{2}{4}$, which is $\frac{1}{2}$.

Tip: Number talks are meant to build fluent retrieval of basic arithmetic facts.

QUESTIONS

- What strategy did you use?
- Does anyone have another strategy to share?
- Can you share your thinking?
- What would happen if...?
- How does this work?

Subtract the fractions using a number line.

$\frac{5}{9} - \frac{2}{9}$	$\frac{6}{8} - \frac{2}{8}$	$\frac{3}{4} - \frac{1}{4}$
$\frac{11}{12} - \frac{5}{12}$	$\frac{5}{7} - \frac{3}{7}$	$\frac{5}{6} - \frac{1}{6}$
$\frac{7}{15} - \frac{2}{15}$	$\frac{4}{5} - \frac{3}{5}$	$\frac{9}{12} - \frac{5}{12}$
$\frac{7}{9} - \frac{4}{9}$	$\frac{6}{7} - \frac{2}{7}$	$\frac{8}{12} - \frac{3}{12}$

Subtracting Fractions Using a Number Line: Unlike Denominators

$$\frac{3}{4} - \frac{2}{3} = ?$$

$$\frac{9}{12} - \frac{8}{12} = \frac{1}{12} \text{ thus } \frac{3}{4} - \frac{2}{3} = \frac{1}{12}$$

You cannot subtract thirds from fourths. But, if you partition both the minuend and subtrahend into 12 parts, you can subtract. Rename $\frac{2}{3}$ as $\frac{8}{12}$ and $\frac{3}{4}$ as $\frac{9}{12}$ and subtract.

Tip: For struggling students, step back to subtracting with like denominators.

QUESTIONS

- Is it possible to subtract $\frac{3}{4}$ and $\frac{2}{3}$?
- How does a number line help you subtract fractions with unlike denominators?

- How can you partition thirds and fourths so they can be subtracted?
- How is this alike or different from subtracting on a number line with like denominators?

Subtract the fractions using a number line.

$\frac{2}{3} - \frac{5}{9}$	$\frac{6}{8} - \frac{2}{4}$	$\frac{3}{4} - \frac{1}{2}$
$\frac{11}{12} - \frac{5}{6}$	$\frac{5}{6} - \frac{2}{3}$	$\frac{5}{6} - \frac{1}{2}$
$\frac{7}{15} - \frac{2}{5}$	$\frac{4}{5} - \frac{1}{10}$	$\frac{9}{10} - \frac{4}{5}$

Subtracting Fractions Using an Area Model: Like Denominators

What is $\frac{6}{8} - \frac{2}{8}$?

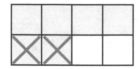

$$\frac{6}{8} - \frac{2}{8} = \frac{4}{8} \ or \ \frac{1}{2}$$

The denominators are the same, so it is easy to subtract. Draw an area model with 8 parts (representing the denominator). You can shade 6 of the parts, then subtract 2 of the eighths.

Tip: If need be, step back to addition of fractions before subtracting.

QUESTIONS

- How do you know how many partitions (equal shapes) you will need?
- How do you know how many eighths will be removed?

- How do you know how many parts to shade?
- Can you share your thinking?

Use an area model to subtract the fractions.

$\frac{8}{10} - \frac{3}{10}$	$\frac{4}{6} - \frac{3}{6}$	$\frac{5}{5} - \frac{3}{5}$
$\frac{5}{8} - \frac{5}{8}$	$\frac{3}{4} - \frac{2}{4}$	$\frac{6}{10} - \frac{1}{10}$
$\frac{8}{11} - \frac{3}{11}$	$\frac{7}{10} - \frac{5}{10}$	$\frac{9}{12} - \frac{3}{12}$
$\frac{10}{11} - \frac{6}{11}$	$\frac{3}{5} - \frac{1}{5}$	$\frac{4}{7} - \frac{2}{7}$

Subtracting Fractions Using an Area Model: Unlike Denominators

$$\frac{2}{3} - \frac{3}{5} = ?$$

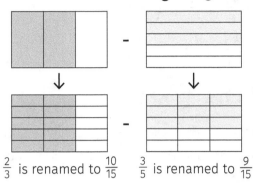

Shaded parts are the numerator. Total parts are the denominator.

Fractions are renamed with a common denominator.

$\frac{2}{3}$ is renamed to $\frac{10}{15}$ $\frac{3}{5}$ is renamed to $\frac{9}{15}$

$$\frac{10}{15} - \frac{9}{15} = \frac{1}{15}. \textit{ Therefore, } \frac{2}{3} - \frac{3}{5} = \frac{1}{15}$$

In order to subtract these two fractions, they must have the same denominator. Begin by making an area model of each fraction. Create a common denominator of 15 by placing the $\frac{2}{3}$ over the $\frac{3}{5}$. This allows you to subtract.

Tip: Fractions can be composed and decomposed to make a new fraction.

QUESTIONS

- What strategy did you use?
- Why can't you add fractions with unlike denominators?
- How do you know how to find a common denominator?
- Can you explain your thinking?

Make an area model of each fraction, then subtract.

$\frac{8}{10} - \frac{3}{5}$	$\frac{8}{12} - \frac{3}{6}$	$\frac{5}{8} - \frac{1}{4}$
$\frac{4}{6} - \frac{1}{3}$	$\frac{3}{4} - \frac{1}{2}$	$\frac{10}{12} - \frac{2}{4}$

Subtracting Fractions Using Decomposition

What is $\dfrac{17}{6} - \dfrac{5}{6}$?

$$\dfrac{12}{6} + \dfrac{5}{6} - \left(\dfrac{5}{6}\right)$$

$$\dfrac{12}{6} + \left(\dfrac{5}{6} - \dfrac{5}{6}\right)$$

$$\dfrac{12}{6} + 0 = \dfrac{12}{6} \text{ or } 2$$

In order to subtract these two fractions, you can decompose $\dfrac{17}{6}$ to make subtraction easier. Since you are subtracting, it is easier to look for zero pairs. You can decompose $\dfrac{17}{6}$ into $\dfrac{12}{6}$ and $\dfrac{5}{6}$. $\dfrac{5}{6} - \dfrac{5}{6}$ will equal 0.

Tip: Scribe student responses and look for more than procedures in discussions.

QUESTIONS

- How would you decompose $\dfrac{17}{6}$ to make subtraction easy?
- Can you show this on a number line?
- What strategy did you use?

- How does this work?
- Can you explain your thinking?
- How do zero pairs help when subtracting fractions?

Decompose to make subtracting the following fractions easier.

$\dfrac{7}{10} - \dfrac{2}{5}$	$\dfrac{9}{12} - \dfrac{2}{6}$	$\dfrac{3}{5} - \dfrac{2}{10}$
$\dfrac{5}{9} - \dfrac{1}{3}$	$\dfrac{4}{6} - \dfrac{2}{3}$	$\dfrac{7}{8} - \dfrac{1}{2}$
$\dfrac{7}{9} - \dfrac{2}{3}$	$\dfrac{6}{8} - \dfrac{2}{4}$	$\dfrac{8}{12} - \dfrac{3}{6}$
$\dfrac{2}{5} - \dfrac{1}{10}$	$\dfrac{5}{9} - \dfrac{3}{6}$	$\dfrac{2}{4} - \dfrac{1}{8}$

Subtracting Fractions Using Equivalency

What is $\frac{2}{3} - \frac{1}{8}$?

Equivalent Fractions

$\frac{4}{6}$ $\frac{6}{9}$ $\frac{8}{12}$ $\frac{10}{15}$ $\frac{12}{18}$ $\frac{5}{13}$ $\boxed{\frac{16}{24}}$

Equivalent Fractions

$\frac{2}{16}$ $\boxed{\frac{3}{24}}$ $\frac{4}{32}$ $\frac{5}{40}$

$$\frac{16}{24} - \frac{3}{24} = \frac{13}{24}$$

You can easily subtract fractions by listing equivalent fractions, then finding the fractions with the same denominators. $\frac{2}{3}$ is equivalent to $\frac{16}{24}$ and $\frac{1}{8}$ is equivalent to $\frac{3}{24}$. $\frac{16}{24} - \frac{3}{24} = \frac{13}{24}$, so $\frac{2}{3} - \frac{1}{8} = \frac{13}{24}$.

Tip: For struggling students, step back to adding with like denominators, or using manipulatives such as fraction tiles or fraction circles.

QUESTIONS

- Can you subtract these fractions without finding a common denominator?
- Can you list equivalent fractions to $\frac{2}{3}$?

- Can you list equivalent fractions to $\frac{1}{8}$?
- Which equivalent fractions have the same denominator?

Subtract using equivalent fractions.

$\frac{2}{5} - \frac{1}{9}$	$\frac{6}{7} - \frac{2}{4}$	$\frac{3}{4} - \frac{1}{3}$
$\frac{11}{12} - \frac{2}{5}$	$\frac{5}{6} - \frac{1}{8}$	$\frac{5}{6} - \frac{2}{4}$
$\frac{7}{9} - \frac{2}{5}$	$\frac{4}{5} - \frac{2}{6}$	$\frac{9}{10} - \frac{3}{8}$
$\frac{7}{9} - \frac{4}{6}$	$\frac{6}{8} - \frac{1}{3}$	$\frac{8}{9} - \frac{2}{7}$

Subtracting Fractions Using Tape Diagrams

EXAMPLE Peter climbed $\frac{3}{8}$ of the way to the top of a mountain on Monday. On Tuesday he climbed $\frac{2}{8}$ more. How much farther does he have to climb to reach the top?

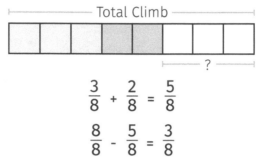

$$\frac{3}{8} + \frac{2}{8} = \frac{5}{8}$$

$$\frac{8}{8} - \frac{5}{8} = \frac{3}{8}$$

You could add $\frac{3}{8}$ and $\frac{2}{8}$ and subtract that sum from $\frac{8}{8}$, or you could subtract both $\frac{3}{8}$ and $\frac{2}{8}$ from $\frac{8}{8}$ to get the solution.

Tip: Students should be solving problems in a way that makes sense to them, just as long as they can explain their reasoning.

QUESTIONS

- How does a tape diagram help you solve this problem?
- What information do you have?
- What information is missing?

- What strategy will you use to find your solution?
- Can you share your strategy with another student?

Use the tape diagram to subtract the fractions.

Ralph spent $\frac{5}{12}$ of his homework time doing math and $\frac{3}{12}$ on science. How much time did he spend on other homework?	Homework Time
Cade spent $\frac{1}{6}$ of her day flying in a plane and $\frac{2}{6}$ of her day visiting her grandmother. What fraction of the day does she have left?	Total Day

Multiplying Fractions Using Repeated Addition

EXAMPLE Mike and Sophie are making cookies. It takes $\frac{2}{3}$ cup of sugar for one batch. If they want to make 3 batches of cookies, how much sugar is needed? Mike likes to think of this as repeated addition. He knows he needs 3 groups of $\frac{2}{3}$ to make 3 batches.

$$3 \times \frac{2}{3} = \frac{2}{3} + \frac{2}{3} + \frac{2}{3} = \frac{6}{3} = 2$$

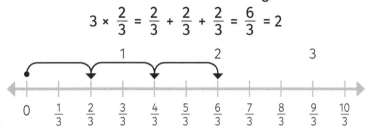

Tip: Students should be solving problems in a way that makes sense to them, just as long as they can explain their reasoning.

QUESTIONS

- How does repeated addition help you multiply?
- How do you know adding will help you find your answer?

- Does anyone have another strategy?
- Can you explain your thinking?

Use repeated addition to multiply fractions.

Quinn loves all kinds of pizza. Her mother had 5 different types of pizzas delivered for a party. Quinn ate $\frac{1}{4}$ of each of the 5 pizzas. How much pizza did Quinn eat?
It takes $\frac{3}{5}$ of a cup of sugar to make one gallon of apple cider. How much sugar would it take to make 6 gallons of cider?
Alan put together a special box of cookies for his friend. He removed $\frac{1}{5}$ of the cookies form 4 different bags. Would he be able to make a full box of cookies?
Laura can read $\frac{3}{5}$ of a novel in a month. If she continues at this rate, how many books can she read in 6 months?

Using Fraction Tiles to Multiply a Whole Number by a Fraction

What is $5 \times \frac{2}{5}$?

1		2		3		4		5	
$\frac{1}{5}$	$\frac{2}{5}$	$\frac{3}{5}$	$\frac{4}{5}$	$\frac{5}{5}$	$\frac{6}{5}$	$\frac{7}{5}$	$\frac{8}{5}$	$\frac{9}{5}$	$\frac{10}{5}$
		1					1		

$$5 \times \frac{2}{5} = 2$$

When multiplying $5 \times \frac{2}{5}$, picture 5 groups of $\frac{2}{5}$. Fraction tiles will help you find an answer. 5 groups of $\frac{2}{5}$ is $\frac{10}{5}$, or 2.

Tip: Number talks are designed to build fluent retrieval of basic arithmetic facts.

QUESTIONS

- What do you see?
- How does this strategy work?
- Can you explain your thinking?
- Does anyone have another strategy?

Multiply the fractions using fractions tiles.

$3 \times \frac{1}{6}$	$5 \times \frac{4}{5}$	$5 \times \frac{1}{2}$
$6 \times \frac{3}{4}$	$3 \times \frac{2}{3}$	$3 \times \frac{2}{10}$
$3 \times \frac{1}{4}$	$6 \times \frac{1}{3}$	$7 \times \frac{2}{5}$
$5 \times \frac{3}{4}$	$2 \times \frac{8}{10}$	$4 \times \frac{2}{6}$
$7 \times \frac{2}{3}$	$5 \times \frac{2}{5}$	$6 \times \frac{5}{6}$

Multiplying a Fraction by a Whole Number

What is $\frac{2}{5} \times 5$

$$\frac{2}{5} + \frac{2}{5} + \frac{2}{5} + \frac{2}{5} + \frac{2}{5} = \frac{10}{5} = 2$$

$$\frac{2}{5} \times 5 = 2$$

When multiplying $\frac{2}{5}$ by 5, picture $\frac{2}{5}$ of 5 groups. Shade in $\frac{2}{5}$ of each of the 5 wholes. Now add the shaded areas together to get 2.

Tip: For struggling learners, use a number line and repeated addition.

QUESTIONS

- How does this strategy work?
- Can you explain your thinking?
- Does anyone have another strategy?
- What happens if you reverse the $\frac{2}{5}$ and 5?

Multiply the fractions.

$\frac{1}{6} \times 3$	$\frac{4}{5} \times 5$	$\frac{4}{8} \times 10$
$\frac{1}{5} \times 4$	$\frac{4}{5} \times 2$	$\frac{4}{6} \times 6$
$\frac{2}{5} \times 7$	$\frac{4}{5} \times 3$	$\frac{2}{3} \times 5$
$\frac{3}{4} \times 4$	$\frac{3}{4} \times 2$	$\frac{3}{8} \times 7$
$\frac{2}{7} \times 3$	$\frac{3}{6} \times 5$	$\frac{2}{5} \times 6$

Multiplying Fractions Using Fraction Tiles and a Number Line

What is $3 \times \frac{1}{4}$?

$\frac{1}{4}$	$\frac{1}{4}$	$\frac{1}{4}$

$$0 \quad \frac{1}{4} \quad \frac{2}{4} \quad \frac{3}{4} \quad 1$$

$$3 \times \frac{1}{4} = \frac{3}{4}$$

When multiplying 3 by $\frac{1}{4}$, you can use fraction tiles and a number line to see that 3 fourths is the same as $\frac{3}{4}$ on a number line.

Tip: Number talks are student driven. They empower students to be mathematically proficient.

QUESTIONS

- Does it help to visualize this problem using fraction tiles?
- What is 3 times $\frac{1}{4}$? Why is it not 12?
- Can you explain your thinking?

Use fractions tiles and a number line to multiply the fractions.

$4 \times \frac{1}{3}$	$7 \times \frac{3}{8}$	$5 \times \frac{3}{6}$
$3 \times \frac{2}{9}$	$5 \times \frac{1}{4}$	$4 \times \frac{1}{8}$
$2 \times \frac{3}{5}$	$4 \times \frac{5}{12}$	$5 \times \frac{1}{2}$
$4 \times \frac{1}{5}$	$6 \times \frac{4}{6}$	$8 \times \frac{5}{8}$

Multiplying Fractions by Whole Numbers Using an Area Model

Brian can eat $\frac{3}{4}$ of a box of cereal for breakfast each day. If he keeps on this schedule, how many boxes of cereal will he need for 4 days?

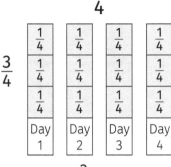

$$4 \times \frac{3}{4} = 3$$

You can picture this by making an area model. Decompose the $\frac{3}{4}$ into unit fractions, so each of the 4 days will show 3 fourths. Four fourths is 1 whole box.

Tip: If students need extra support, step back to addition of fractions.

QUESTIONS

- What do you see?
- How does this strategy work?
- Can you explain this in your own words?

- What questions do you have?
- Is there anything you still do not understand?

Multiply using an area model.

Carter made homemade granola for his family. He expects each of his 5 family members to eat $\frac{2}{3}$ of a bowl. How much granola should he make?		
$5 \times \frac{5}{6}$	$4 \times \frac{7}{8}$	$5 \times \frac{4}{9}$
$2 \times \frac{9}{12}$	$6 \times \frac{4}{5}$	$3 \times \frac{2}{7}$

Multiplying Fractions Using an Area Model (Fraction × Fraction)

$$\frac{3}{4} \times \frac{1}{2} = ?$$

Shade 3 out of 4 columns
for the first fraction

Draw lines
through 1 out
of 2 rows for
the second
fraction

Three out of the 8 total boxes are shaded and have a pattern through them. The product is $\frac{3}{8}$, which is represented by the dark outlined region. You can see the number of parts (3) and the whole (8).

Tip: For struggling learners, have fraction tiles, fraction strips, or fraction circles available that they can hold and manipulate.

QUESTIONS

- What do you see?
- How does this strategy work?

- Why shade 3 out of 4 and 1 out of 2?
- Will this work for all fractions?

Multiply using an area model.

$\frac{5}{8} \times \frac{2}{10}$	$\frac{1}{4} \times \frac{1}{5}$	$\frac{6}{8} \times \frac{1}{2}$
$\frac{1}{3} \times \frac{5}{6}$	$\frac{2}{3} \times \frac{3}{4}$	$\frac{2}{5} \times \frac{2}{3}$
$\frac{1}{9} \times \frac{2}{7}$	$\frac{1}{4} \times \frac{4}{7}$	$\frac{2}{8} \times \frac{1}{2}$

Multiplying Fractions by Fractions Using Counters

EXAMPLE

$$\frac{3}{5} \times \frac{2}{3} = ?$$

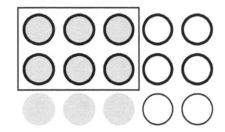

Three out of five columns are shaded for the first fraction. Two out of three rows are highlighted for the second fraction. The product is $\frac{6}{15}$, or $\frac{2}{5}$.

Tip: Before using a traditional approach, try a visual approach such as counters or an area model.

QUESTIONS

- What do you see?
- How does this strategy work?
- How do you know which counters to shade?
- How to you determine the product?

Use counters to multiply the following fractions.

$\frac{2}{3} \times \frac{3}{5}$	$\frac{1}{3} \times \frac{2}{4}$	$\frac{1}{8} \times \frac{3}{4}$
$\frac{1}{5} \times \frac{2}{3}$	$\frac{3}{4} \times \frac{2}{6}$	$\frac{7}{8} \times \frac{1}{3}$
$\frac{5}{7} \times \frac{1}{3}$	$\frac{1}{9} \times \frac{1}{4}$	$\frac{2}{8} \times \frac{2}{3}$
$\frac{3}{8} \times \frac{1}{5}$	$\frac{1}{2} \times \frac{1}{2}$	$\frac{3}{7} \times \frac{2}{7}$

Multiplying Fractions Using Tape Diagrams

EXAMPLE There are 80 students in Mr. Bill's class. If $\frac{3}{5}$ of them went on a field trip, how many were left?

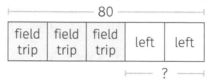

$$\frac{80}{5} \times 2 = 32$$

Each unit is 16 students because 80 divided by 5 is 16, so the number of students going on the field trip would be 16 x 3, or 48 students, but the ones remaining would be 16 x 2, or 32 students.

Tip: Students should be able to use an algorithm but also model, estimate, and explain their reasoning.

QUESTIONS

- What do you see?
- What is the problem asking?
- How can you solve this problem?

- What strategy will you use?
- What does your answer mean?

Chris had 25 apps on his iPad. He deleted $\frac{2}{5}$ of the apps. How many did he delete? 	Stephen bought 16 songs on iTunes. If $\frac{1}{8}$ of the songs didn't load correctly, how many songs were loaded correctly? 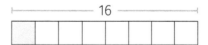
Peter purchased 15 pizzas for a party. He made sure that $\frac{1}{5}$ of the pizzas were cheese only. How many pizzas were cheese? 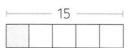	Manny spent 3 hours playing "Words with Friends." $\frac{1}{4}$ of the time he played with Susan and the rest of the time with Ken. How much time did he spend playing with Susan?

Multiplying Fractions Using the Distributive Property

Find $10 \times \frac{2}{5}$

$(10 \times \frac{1}{5}) + (10 \times \frac{1}{5}) = 2 + 2 = 4$

or

$(5 \times \frac{2}{5}) + (5 \times \frac{2}{5}) = 2 + 2 = 4$

Use the distributive property to look for friendlier multiplication expressions. You can write and choose between two different expressions to find the same answer.

Tip: Provide adequate time to explore multiplication of fractions conceptually.

QUESTIONS

- What do you see?
- How are these two expressions alike?
- How are the answers the same?

- How does the distributive property help make multiplication friendlier?

Use the distributive property to multiply the fractions.

$6 \times \frac{2}{3}$	$8 \times \frac{3}{4}$	$10 \times \frac{2}{5}$
$12 \times \frac{2}{6}$	$12 \times \frac{2}{3}$	$14 \times \frac{2}{7}$
$16 \times \frac{3}{8}$	$16 \times \frac{3}{4}$	$16 \times \frac{7}{8}$
$10 \times \frac{4}{5}$	$8 \times \frac{2}{4}$	$18 \times \frac{2}{9}$

Finding Perimeter Using
$P = 2l + 2w$ or $P = 2(l + w)$

EXAMPLE

What is the perimeter of this shape?

3 units

$\frac{3}{4}$

$\frac{1}{4}$	$\frac{1}{4}$	$\frac{1}{4}$
$\frac{1}{4}$	$\frac{1}{4}$	$\frac{1}{4}$
$\frac{1}{4}$	$\frac{1}{4}$	$\frac{1}{4}$

$$P = 2\left(\frac{3}{4}\right) + 2(3)$$

$$P = 1\frac{1}{2} + 6$$

$$P = 7\frac{1}{2} \text{ units}$$

$$P = 2\left(\frac{3}{4} + 3\right)$$

$$P = 2\left(3\frac{3}{4}\right)$$

$$P = 7\frac{1}{2} \text{ units}$$

You can find the perimeter by multiplying both length and width by 2 and then adding the products, or adding the length and width together first and then multiplying by 2.

Tip: For the struggling learner, use a concrete model like a geoboard and have students count the side lengths. You can also step back to simply adding all sides to find the perimeter.

QUESTIONS

- Is this similar to another strategy you know?

- What strategy did you use to find perimeter? Explain.

- What would happen if you double the sides and add?

- Will you get the same answer if you add the two sides and then double the answer? Why does this work?

What is the perimeter of this shape?

20 units $\frac{4}{5}$ unit	15 units $\frac{2}{3}$ unit	70 units $\frac{7}{10}$ unit
8 units $\frac{3}{4}$ unit	50 units $\frac{6}{10}$ unit	30 units $\frac{2}{15}$ unit

Area: $A = lw$

What is the area of the shape below?

$\frac{3}{4}$ mile

$\frac{4}{5}$ mile

$$\frac{3}{4} \times \frac{4}{5} = \frac{12}{20} \text{ or } \frac{3}{5}$$

To find the area of this shape, shade 3 out of 4 squares for the first factor and 4 out of 5 squares for the second factor. There are now a total of 20 squares. The overlap of the two shaded regions shows the solution. $\frac{12}{20}$, or in simple terms, $\frac{3}{5}$.

Tip: For a struggling learner, have them use a geoboard or geoboard paper to construct the shape. Have the student count the squares that make up the shape to find the area.

QUESTIONS

- How can you find the area of this shape without counting the squares?

- What strategy did you use to find the area of this shape?

- Would anyone like to share a different strategy?

What is the area of this shape?

$\frac{5}{6}$ unit / $\frac{4}{5}$ unit	$\frac{4}{6}$ unit / $\frac{2}{3}$ unit	$\frac{3}{4}$ unit / $\frac{7}{10}$ unit
$\frac{7}{9}$ unit / $\frac{3}{4}$ unit	$\frac{2}{6}$ unit / $\frac{6}{10}$ unit	$\frac{1}{3}$ unit / $\frac{2}{15}$ unit

Dividing a Whole Number by a Unit Fraction Using Part-Part-Whole Model

What is $2 \div \frac{1}{4}$?

$$2 \div \frac{1}{4} = 8$$

1			
$\frac{1}{4}$	$\frac{1}{4}$	$\frac{1}{4}$	$\frac{1}{4}$

2			
$\frac{1}{4}$	$\frac{1}{4}$	$\frac{1}{4}$	$\frac{1}{4}$

How many quarters are in 2 wholes? You can understand this by drawing a part-part-whole model. There are 8 fourths in 2 wholes.

Tip: Help students understand why their strategy or a particular strategy makes sense.

QUESTIONS

- What do you see?
- Do you have a strategy you want to share?
- What questions do you have?
- Can you explain this strategy to your classmate?

Draw a Part-Part-Whole Model and solve.

$1 \div \frac{1}{2}$	$2 \div \frac{1}{5}$	$1 \div \frac{1}{12}$
$2 \div \frac{1}{7}$	$2 \div \frac{1}{9}$	$2 \div \frac{1}{3}$
$1 \div \frac{1}{9}$	$3 \div \frac{1}{12}$	$2 \div \frac{1}{3}$
$3 \div \frac{1}{6}$	$4 \div \frac{1}{3}$	$4 \div \frac{1}{6}$

Dividing a Whole Number by a Unit Fraction

What is $5 \div \frac{1}{4}$?

$$5 \div \frac{1}{4} = 20$$

1   2   3   4   5

You can visualize this problem using a model. Begin by drawing 5 wholes. Once you have the 5 wholes, partition each whole into 4 parts. There are 4 parts in 1 whole, so there are 20 fourths in 5 wholes.

Tip: Before introducing the algorithm for dividing fractions, have students explore conceptual models.

QUESTIONS

- How many fourths are in 5 wholes?
- How many fourths are in 1 whole?

- Does drawing a model help with understanding?
- Can you explain your strategy?

Draw a model and solve.

$6 \div \frac{1}{3}$	$4 \div \frac{1}{8}$	$5 \div \frac{1}{5}$
$3 \div \frac{1}{9}$	$7 \div \frac{1}{7}$	$3 \div \frac{1}{6}$
$4 \div \frac{1}{9}$	$6 \div \frac{1}{7}$	$4 \div \frac{1}{3}$
$3 \div \frac{1}{10}$	$5 \div \frac{1}{11}$	$7 \div \frac{1}{5}$

Dividing a Unit Fraction by a Whole Number

What is $\frac{1}{5} \div 3$?

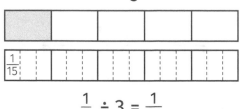

$$\frac{1}{5} \div 3 = \frac{1}{15}$$

Visualize this problem using a model. Begin by partitioning a whole into 5 equal parts, representing the dividend. Look at the value of the shaded piece in respect to the whole—this is $\frac{1}{5}$. You need to partition $\frac{1}{5}$ into 3 parts. The value of each $\frac{1}{5}$ piece, once it is partitioned, is $\frac{1}{15}$, the quotient. So, when $\frac{1}{5}$ is partitioned into 3 equal groups, each piece is $\frac{1}{15}$.

Tip: Students need more than a simple algorithm to divide fractions. To truly understand, rely on more than "invert and multiply".

QUESTIONS

- What do you see?
- How does this model work?
- Can you think of a real-life situation using this equation?

- Why do we begin by partitioning into 5 equal parts?
- Why do we partition each part into 3 additional parts?

Draw a model and solve.

$\frac{1}{2} \div 3$	$\frac{1}{5} \div 4$	$\frac{1}{2} \div 2$
$\frac{1}{8} \div 2$	$\frac{1}{2} \div 6$	$\frac{1}{7} \div 6$
$\frac{1}{3} \div 4$	$\frac{1}{8} \div 3$	$\frac{1}{6} \div 6$

Dividing a Unit Fraction by a Whole Number Using a Number Line

What is $\frac{1}{5} \div 3$?

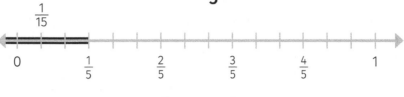

$$\frac{1}{5} \div 3 = \frac{1}{15}$$

How many groups of 3 are in $\frac{1}{5}$? Begin by drawing a number line from 0 to 1 and partitioning it into fifths. You can find how many groups of 3 are in $\frac{1}{5}$ by dividing each fifth into 3. Instead of having 5 partitions, you now have 15 equal parts. The value of each piece now is $\frac{1}{15}$, the quotient. So, when $\frac{1}{5}$ is partitioned into 3 equal groups, each piece is $\frac{1}{15}$.

Tip: For struggling learners, step back to division by whole numbers.

QUESTIONS

- What do you see?
- How does this model work?
- Can you think of a real-life situation using this equation?

- Why do we begin by partitioning one whole into 5 equal parts?
- Why do we partition each fifth into 3 additional parts?

Use a number line to solve.

$\frac{1}{2} \div 3$	$\frac{1}{5} \div 4$	$\frac{1}{2} \div 2$
$\frac{1}{8} \div 2$	$\frac{1}{2} \div 6$	$\frac{1}{7} \div 6$
$\frac{1}{3} \div 4$	$\frac{1}{8} \div 3$	$\frac{1}{6} \div 6$

Dividing a Whole Number by a Unit Fraction Using a Number Line

What is $3 \div \frac{1}{4}$?

1	2	3	4	5	6	7	8	9	10	11	12

$0 \quad \frac{1}{4} \quad \frac{2}{4} \quad \frac{3}{4} \quad 1 \quad 1\frac{1}{4} \quad 1\frac{2}{4} \quad 1\frac{3}{4} \quad 2 \quad 2\frac{1}{4} \quad 2\frac{2}{4} \quad 2\frac{3}{4} \quad 3$

$$3 \div \frac{1}{4} = 12$$

How many fourths are there in 3 wholes? Begin by drawing a number line and partitioning it into three wholes. You can find how many groups of $\frac{1}{4}$ are in 3 wholes by dividing each whole into fourths. You now have 12 equal parts.

Tip: For understanding, have students draw pictures, models, or number lines to make sense of division.

QUESTIONS

- How does this model work?
- Can you think of a real-life situation using this equation?

- Why do we begin by partitioning into 3 equal parts?
- Why do we partition each part into 4 additional parts?

Use a number line to solve.

$6 \div \frac{1}{3}$	$4 \div \frac{1}{8}$	$5 \div \frac{1}{5}$
$3 \div \frac{1}{9}$	$7 \div \frac{1}{7}$	$3 \div \frac{1}{6}$
$4 \div \frac{1}{9}$	$6 \div \frac{1}{7}$	$4 \div \frac{1}{3}$
$3 \div \frac{1}{10}$	$5 \div \frac{1}{11}$	$7 \div \frac{1}{5}$

Dividing a Whole Number by a Fraction

Lanie bought 3 large pizzas for her party. If she wants each friend to get 3/5 of a pizza, how many friends can she invite?

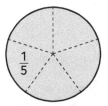 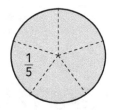 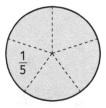

Lanie can invite 5 friends.

Tip: Students determine an answer to a number talk mentally giving a thumbs-up when they have an answer.

QUESTIONS

- What do you see?
- What operation will help you solve this problem?
- What number sentence can be used?

- What is the solution to this problem?
- What strategy did you use?

Degan made 5 pies for his party. Degan wanted each guest to have $\frac{1}{8}$ of a pie. How many guests could Degan invite to his party?

A chef has 6 cups of sugar. Each cake he makes requires $\frac{1}{2}$ cup of sugar. How many cakes can he make with 6 cups of sugar?

Decimals

"Mathematics is the art of giving the same name to different things."

—*Henri Poincaré*

5.NBT.B.7 Add, subtract, multiply, and divide decimals to hundredths, using concrete models or drawings and strategies based on place value, properties of operations, and/or the relationship between addition and subtraction; relate the strategy to a written method and explain the reasoning used.

In this section are the following decimal strategy worksheets:

Identifying Decimals

Identify the decimal.

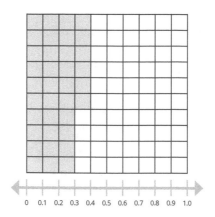

36 out of the 100 squares are shaded (36/100). You can use the number line, as well, to help identify the decimal as 0.36 (thirty-six hundredths).

Tip: Try to make sure the number talk is student driven, not teacher directed.

QUESTIONS

- How do you identify the decimal shown?
- What decimal is shown?

- How many squares are shaded?
- How do you say the decimal in words?

What decimal is represented?

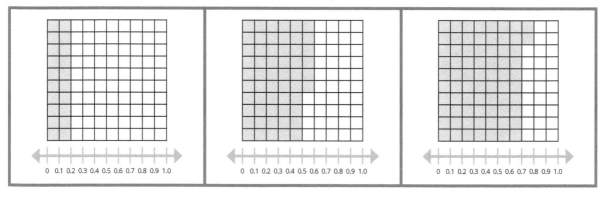

Decimal Place Value

Identify the decimal.

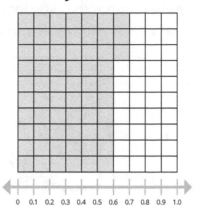

Word form: six tenths and three hundredths

Expanded Form: 0.60 + 0.03

You can tell that there are 6 tenths and 3 hundredths because 6 complete columns (0.60) and 3 additional squares (0.03) have been shaded.

Tip: Encourage students to think about mathematics in a way that makes sense to them.

QUESTIONS

- How do you identify the decimal shown?
- What decimal is shown?

- How many squares are shaded?
- What is the word name for this decimal?

Identify the decimals in word form and expanded form.

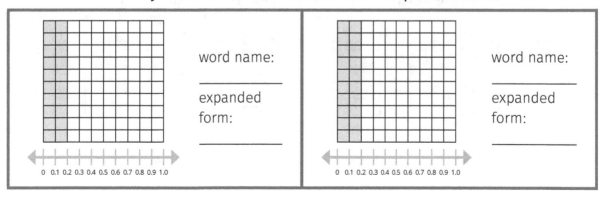

word name:

_____

expanded form:

_____

word name:

_____

expanded form:

_____

Rounding Decimals to the Nearest Whole

Using the hundredths charts, round 1.46 to the nearest whole number. Is 1.46 closer to the whole number 1 or the whole number 2?

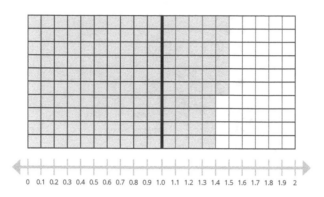

You can see here that 1 whole is shaded (10 columns, or 1.00), along with 4 complete columns (0.40) and 6 additional squares (0.06 hundredths), which would equal 1.46. This is less than halfway to 2 wholes, so you would round 1.46 to the nearest whole number, which is 1.

Tip: Through these number talks, students learn by listening to strategies shared by others.

QUESTIONS

- How do you identify the decimal shown?
- What decimal is shown?
- How many squares are shaded?
- Is this decimal number closer to 1 or 2?

Identify the decimals and round them to the nearest whole.

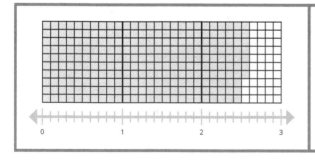 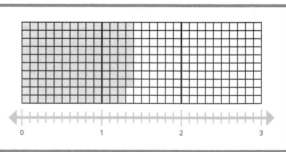

Adding Decimals Using Decimal Squares

0.45 + 0.71 = ?

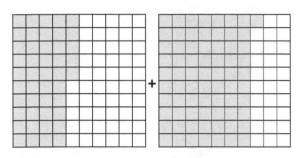

0.45 + 0.71 = 1.16

You can use decimal squares to add two decimals. The first addend has 4 columns, or 0.40, and the second addend has 7 columns, which is 0.70. Together, that is 1.10. There are also 6 additional squares, which is 6 hundredths (0.06). So, the final sum is 1.16.

Tip: Encourage students to see that there are many different ways to solve a problem.

QUESTIONS

- How many squares are shaded in the first addend (square)?
- How many squares are shaded in the second addend (square)?
- How do you get your sum?
- Can you explain your thinking?

Find the sum.

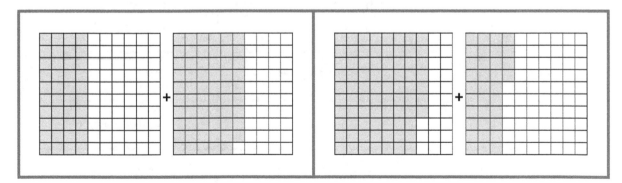

Adding Decimals by Decomposing (Partial Sums)

12.45 + 4.62 = ?

12.45 + 4.00 = 16.45

16.45 + 0.60 = 17.05

17.05 + 0.02 = 17.07

Decompose the second addend to make addition easier. First, add the whole number (4.00), then add on the number in the tenths place (0.60), and finally the number in the hundredths place (0.02).

Tip: Try to make sure the number talk is student driven, not teacher directed.

QUESTIONS

- What strategy did you use? Can you explain your strategy?
- Can you give me another example?

How can you decompose the decimals before adding?

35.41 + 4.73	12.65 + 8.45	46.28 + 8.47
23.64 + 12.57	56.42 + 9.51	24.74 + 6.76
18.45 + 7.54	58.37 + 6.44	63.21 + 5.76
22.83 + 21.58	69.37 + 4.71	28.92 + 2.53
78.45 + 4.26	20.05 + 8.36	92.64 + 8.23
48.93 + 1.43	88.42 + 2.56	75.49 + 3.53

Adding Decimals Using a Place Value Strategy

$$10.48 + 5.32 = ?$$
$$10 + 0.4 + 0.08$$
$$5 + 0.3 + 0.02$$
$$15 + 0.7 + 0.10 = 15.80$$

You can add these decimals by decomposing by place values and then using vertical addition. Add the whole numbers, the tenths, and finally the hundredths. The final sum is 15.80.

Tip: For struggling learners, start with decomposing whole numbers.

QUESTIONS

- How can you decompose these numbers to made addition easier?
- Can you explain how these numbers are added?
- What strategy did you use?
- Does anyone have a different strategy they want to share?

Decompose the decimals by place value and add.

10.45 + 6.23	5.67 + 3.24	3.56 + 8.27
1.45 + 6.74	2.89 + 3.46	12.57 + 13.28
16.49 + 21.34	7.72 + 9.47	26.12 + 12.82
52.34 + 41.61	8.91 + 6.34	12.63 + 7.25
8.91 + 7.02	1.06 + 12.33	7.35 + 6.28
4.231 + 2.11	6.372 + 4.21	8.541 + 7.65

Adding Decimals on an Open Number Line

3.25 + 4.37 = ?

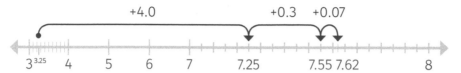

Begin at 3.25, jump 4 whole numbers to 7.25, jump 3 tenths more to 7.55, and then finally jump 7 hundredths to 7.62, which is the sum of both decimals.

Tip: It is important that students find a strategy that makes sense to them and a strategy they understand.

QUESTIONS

- How can you describe this strategy?
- Can you share with your neighbor?
- Why jump by a whole, tenth, and hundredth?

- What other strategy could you use?
- Is this similar to any other strategies you know?

Use a number line to add the decimals.

6.35 + 2.89	0.89 + 1.25	5.61 + 7.02
1.52 + 2.3	2.08 + 3.21	6.24 + 8.05
4.46 + 3.52	5.46 + 0.19	8.82 + 2.14
7.23 + 2.16	3.53 + 1.11	2.47 + 6.41
0.99 + 0.24	1.89 + 0.24	5.82 + 2.64
4.46 + 2.85	6.37 + 4.21	8.54 + 7.65

Adding Decimals in Expanded Form

$$7.42 \quad + \quad 8.75 = ?$$

$$(7 + 0.4 + 0.02) + (8 + 0.7 + 0.05)$$

$$(7 + 8) + (0.4 + 0.7) + (0.02 + 0.05)$$

$$15 + 1.1 + 0.07 = 16.17$$

You can add the decimals by decomposing by place values. Then add the whole numbers (7 + 8), the tenths (0.4 + 0.7), and finally the hundredths (0.02 + 0.05). Now, combine the sums for a final value of 16.17.

Tip: For struggling learners, use decimal tiles or a hundreds chart and have the students shade the value.

QUESTIONS

- How can you decompose these numbers to made addition easier?
- How does this work?

- Can you explain how these numbers are added?
- What strategy did you use?

Write the decimals in expanded form and add.

6.35 + 2.89	0.89 + 1.25	5.61 + 7.02
1.52 + 2.3	2.08 + 3.21	6.24 + 8.05
4.46 + 3.52	5.46 + 0.19	8.82 + 2.14
7.23 + 2.16	3.53 + 1.11	2.47 + 6.41
0.99 + 0.24	1.89 + 1.62	5.82 + 2.64
4.46 + 2.85	6.37 + 4.21	8.54 + 7.65

Subtracting Decimals by Counting Back by Ones, Tenths, and Hundredths

EXAMPLE

$$10.58 - 5.32 = ?$$

$$10.58 - 5.00 = 5.58$$

$$5.58 - 0.10 - 0.10 - 0.10 = 5.28$$

$$5.28 - 0.01 - 0.01 = 5.26$$

Begin by subtracting the whole number 5 from the minuend 10.58 to get a difference of 5.58. Now you can subtract the tenths (0.30, or three sets of 0.10). Finally, subtract the hundredths (0.02, or 2 sets of 0.01). The final difference is 5.26.

Tip: Encourage students to share their strategies conceptually instead of using a procedure.

QUESTIONS

- What strategy did you use? Can you explain your strategy?
- Can you give me another example?

Subtract the decimals by counting back.

15.76 - 10.32	12.65 - 2.14	16.28 - 8.21
23.64 - 12.34	26.42 - 9.21	24.74 - 6.33
18.45 - 7.34	28.37 - 6.24	63.21 - 35.11
22.83 - 21.22	19.37 - 8.21	28.92 - 2.21
18.45 - 4.25	20.05 - 8.03	12.64 - 8.23
18.93 - 1.43	8.42 - 2.31	15.49 - 3.24

Subtracting Decimals on an Open Number Line

7.46 – 4.21 = ?

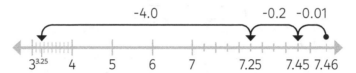

Begin on an open number line at 7.46 and jump back one hundredth to 7.45. Then, jump back 2 tenths to 7.25, and finally, jump back 4 wholes to 3.25, the final answer.

Tip: For struggling learners, add with whole numbers on an open number line.

QUESTIONS

- Can you describe this strategy?
- Could I have measured the distance between 4.21 and 7.46 and gotten the same solution?
- Can you share your thinking?

Subtract the decimals by counting back on a number line.

5.67 – 3.24	8.97 – 2.45	7.68 – 2.21
10.67 – 5.23	12.42 – 9.21	4.74 – 1.33
9.34 – 7.20	18.37 – 5.27	21.21 – 13.11
5.83 – 1.22	9.87 – 8.21	4.92 – 2.71
1.45 – 0.23	10.05 – 2.03	2.64 – 1.23
8.93 – 6.42	8.42 + 7.31	15.49 – 12.26

Subtracting Decimals Using Decimal Squares

0.78 - 0.35 = ?

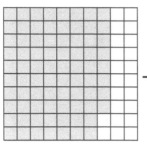 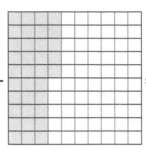

0.78 - 0.35 = 0.43

You need to subtract the subtrahend (0.35) from the minuend (0.78). The subtrahend is made of 3 columns (0.30, or 30/100), which you can remove from the minuend, along with an additional 5 squares (0.05, or 5/100). The difference is what is left, which is 43 out of 100 (0.43).

Tip: Number talks help students deeply learn math instead of learning a set of rules and procedures without the conceptual understanding.

QUESTIONS

- How many squares are shaded in the minuend?
- How many squares are shaded in the subtrahend?
- How do you find the difference?
- Can you explain your thinking?

Find the difference.

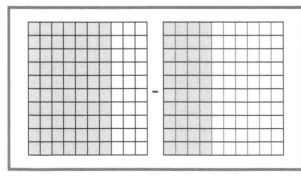 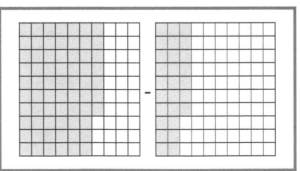

Subtracting Decimals Using a Place Value Strategy: No Regrouping

$$10.58 - 5.32 = ?$$

$$
\begin{array}{r}
10 + 0.5 + 0.08 \\
- \quad 5 + 0.3 + 0.02 \\
\hline
5 + 0.2 + 0.06 = 5.26
\end{array}
$$

You can subtract these decimals by decomposing by place values and vertical subtraction. First subtract the whole numbers, then the tenths, and finally the hundredths. The final difference is 5.26.

Tip: Mistakes are an opportunity for discussion.

QUESTIONS

- How does place value help you subtract decimals?
- Can you explain your strategy?
- Do you need to see this a different way?
- Is this strategy similar to another strategy you have used?

Decompose place values and subtract the decimals.

9.43 - 5.21	12.78 - 7.46	15.98 - 10.83
3.76 - 0.54	8.95 - 1.53	7.94 - 2.71
25.87 - 11.64	43.59 - 20.46	8.82 - 4.72
13.69 - 10.37	12.65 - 7.22	16.88 - 8.57
4.68 - 0.47	2.99 - 0.74	8.27 - 3.16
27.75 - 12.42	45.54 - 32.22	7.79 - 2.56

Multiplying Decimals Using Decimal Squares

0.36 × 4 = ?

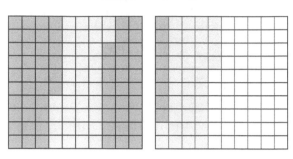

0.36 × 4 = 1.44

Multiplying 0.36 by 4 is like adding 0.36 four times on a decimal square (repeated addition). The product is the total of the shaded region, or 1.44 (one and 44 hundredths).

Tip: For struggling learners, use decimal squares or a hundreds chart and have the student shade the value and count the squares.

QUESTIONS

- How many times will you shade 0.36?
- How does this work?
- Can you explain the product in your own words?

- How does this strategy work?
- How is this like multiplying whole numbers?

Use decimal squares to multiply the decimals.

0.42 × 3	0.12 × 4	0.36 × 2
0.41 × 2	0.42 × 3	0.11 × 3
0.35 × 3	0.45 × 3	0.51 × 2
0.14 × 5	0.26 × 4	0.33 × 2

Multiplying Decimals Using Decimal Squares with an Array

0.5 × 0.3 = ?

0.5

0.3

0.5 × 0.3 = 0.15

You can multiply by using an array. Shade 0.5, or the first 5 columns of the decimal square. Then put x's over 0.3, which is the first 3 rows on the decimal square. The product is the area where the x's and shades overlap.

Tip: For struggling learners, step back to whole number multiplication using an array.

QUESTIONS

- How do you shade both factors?
- How do you know the product using a decimal square?
- Can you explain this strategy?
- Can you share your thinking with another student?

Use an array to multiply.

0.6 × 0.4	0.9 × 0.7	0.4 × 0.7
0.5 × 0.3	0.2 × 0.8	0.1 × 0.9
0.1 × 0.5	0.4 × 0.9	0.2 × 0.5
0.1 × 0.8	0.2 × 0.3	0.4 × 0.7

Multiplying Decimals Using an Area Model

EXAMPLE

1.38 × 3.7 = ?

	1 +	0.3 +	0.08
3	3	0.9	0.24
+ 0.7	0.7	0.21	0.056

3 + 0.9 + 0.7 + 0.24 + 0.21 + 0.056 = 5.106

Begin by decomposing the 2 factors. Multiply 3 by 1, 0.3, and 0.08. Then, multiply 0.7 by 1, 0.3, and 0.08. Finally, add all the products within the rectangle to get the product.

Tip: For struggling learners, start with an area model with whole numbers only.

QUESTIONS

- How is this area model similar to the area model with whole numbers?
- Can you explain this strategy?
- How do you decompose the factors in this area model?
- How does this make multiplication easier?

Use an area model to multiply the decimals.

3.45 × 2.5	5.23 × 1.2	4.82 × 0.7
6.45 × 2.2	9.21 × 3.4	1.15 × 0.6
2.64 × 4.3	7.26 × 0.5	8.81 × 1.6
3.27 × 3.1	5.58 × 2.4	4.25 × 1.5
6.62 × 3.4	9.12 × 0.4	1.68 × 1.2
6.52 × 4.6	3.91 × 41	5.55 × 2.6

Dividing Decimals Using Decimal Squares

3.60 ÷ 1.20 = ?

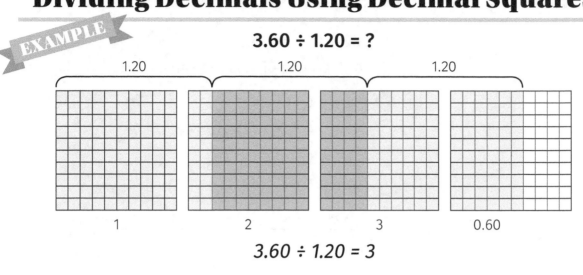

3.60 ÷ 1.20 = 3

You can divide these 2 decimals by asking, "How many 1.20s are there in 3.60?" You can show this by using 3 whole squares and 6 columns from a fourth whole square, which equals 3.60, and shading in each set of 1.20. From the shading, you see that there are exactly three 1.20s in 3.60.

Tip: A number talk should be about how you go about solving and explaining the problem.

QUESTIONS

- How can you show this division?
- What do you think would happen if you had more or less than 3.60?
- Can you show this problem using a model?
- How is this like other problems you have solved?

Use decimal squares to divide.

4.8 ÷ 1.2	0.75 ÷ 5	1.2 ÷ 0.4
5.2 ÷ 10	3.6 ÷ 4	2.4 ÷ 0.6
3.2 ÷ 0.8	2.1 ÷ 0.3	4.2 ÷ 0.6

Dividing Decimals Based on Multiplication

3.2 ÷ 0.4 = ?

Known: 8 x 4 = 32, or 8 groups of 4, is the same as

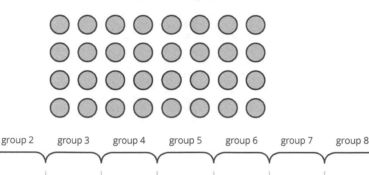

| group 1 | group 2 | group 3 | group 4 | group 5 | group 6 | group 7 | group 8 |

Thus, 8 groups of 0.4 will be 3.2 or 8 x 0.4 = 3.2

Begin by asking yourself, "How many groups of 0.4 are in 3.2?" You know that 8 groups of 4 is 32, or 8 x 4 = 32. Because 8 groups of 4 is 32, you know that 8 groups of 0.4 is 3.2. Therefore, 8 x 0.4 = 3.2. Understanding related facts, you can conclude that 3.2 ÷ 4 = 8.

Tip: For struggling learners, review division by whole numbers based on multiplication facts.

QUESTIONS

- How does multiplication of whole numbers relate to division of whole numbers?

- How do related facts help you divide decimals?

- How can you divide decimals based on multiplication?

- What other groups do you see?

Use multiplication facts to solve.

3.3 ÷ 0.3	4.5 ÷ 0.5	7.2 ÷ 0.6
4.9 ÷ 0.7	3.2 ÷ 0.4	5.6 ÷ 0.8
3.6 ÷ 0.9	8.4 ÷ 1.2	2.4 ÷ 0.2

Further Reading Opportunities

National Governors Association Center for Best Practices and Council of Chief State School Officers. *Common Core State Standards for Mathematics*. Washington, DC: National Governors Association Center for Best Practices and Council of Chief State School Officers, 2010.

Van de Walle, John, Karen S. Karp, LouAnn H. Lovin, and Jennifer M. Bay-Williams. *Teaching Student-Centered Mathematics: Developmentally Appropriate Instruction for Grades 3–5*. 2nd ed. London, England: Pearson, 2013.

Parrish, Sherry. *Number Talks: Helping Children Build Mental Math and Computation Strategies, Grades K–5*. Sausalito, CA: Math Solutions, 2010.

Humphreys, Cathy, and Ruth Parker. *Making Number Talks Matter. Developing Mathematical Practices and Deepening Understanding, Grades 4–10*. Portland, ME: Stenhouse Publishers, 2015.

References

Boaler, Jo. *Mathematical Mindsets: Unleashing Students' Potential through Creative Math, Inspiring Messages, and Innovative Teaching.* San Francisco, CA: Jossey-Bass, 2016.

Chapin, Suzanne, Catherine O'Connor, and Nancy Canavan Anderson. *Classroom Discussions: Using Math to Help Students Learn.* Sausalito, CA: Math Solutions, 2009.

Common Core. "Common Core State Standards Initiative." www.corestandards.org.

Diller, Debbie. *Math Work Stations:* Independent *Learning You Can Count On.* Portland, ME: Stenhouse, 2011.

Forsten, Char, and Torri Richards. *Math Talk: Teaching Concepts and Skills through Illustrations and Stories.* Peterborough, NH: Crystal Springs, 2009.

Humphreys, Cathy and Ruth Parker. *Making Number Talks Matter: Developing Mathematical Practices and Deepening Understanding, Grades 4-10.* Portland, ME: Stenhouse, 2015.

Ma, Liping. *Knowing and Teaching Elementary Mathematics.* Mahwah, NH: Erlbaum, 1999.

McNamara, Julie and Meghan M. Shaughnessy. *Beyond Pizzas and Pies: 10 Essential Strategies for Supporting Fraction Section.* Sausalito, CA: Math Solutions, 2015.

O'Connell, Susan and John SanGiovanni. *Mastering the Basic Math Facts in Addition and Subtraction: Strategies, Activities and Interventions to Move Students Beyond Memorization.* Portsmouth, NH: Heinemann, 2011.

Parrish, Sherry. *Number Talks: Whole Number Computation, Grades K-5.* Sausalito, CA: Math Solutions, 2010.

Shumway, Jessica F. *Number Sense Routines: Building Numerical Literacy Every Day in Grades K-3.* Portland, ME: Stenhouse, 2011.

Van de Walle, John A., Karen S. Karp, LouAnn H. Lovin, and Jennifer Bay-Williams. *Teaching Student-Centered Mathematics: Developmentally Appropriate Instruction for Grades 3-5.* New York, NY: Pearson, 2014.

Van de Walle, John A., Karen S. Karp, and Jennifer Bay-Williams. *Elementary and Middle School Mathematics: Teaching Developmentally.* Harlow, UK: Pearson, 2015.

About the Author

Nancy Hughes spent the last 10 years as K–12 mathematics coordinator at Olathe Public Schools, the largest school district in the Kansas City region, where she also provided professional development for mathematics teachers in all grade levels. Prior to working in Olathe, Hughes taught middle school math in Kansas City area public and private schools. Hughes has presented math topics at conferences for the National Council of Teachers of Mathematics, Kansas City Area Teachers of Mathematics, and Kansas Area Teachers of Mathematics. She also directed the Kauffman Foundation's K–16 Professional Development program. Hughes has a B.S. from Kansas State University and an M.S. in Curriculum and Instruction from Kansas University.